Imogen Stubbs

WE HAPPY FEW

NICK HERN BOOKS
London
www.nickhernbooks.co.uk

A Nick Hern Book

We Happy Few first published in as a paperback original in 2004 by
Nick Hern Books Limited, 14 Larden Road, London W3 7ST

Reprinted 2008, 2009, 2011

We Happy Few copyright © 2004 Imogen Stubbs

'In Search of the Osiris Players'
copyright © 2004 Fred Moroni and Louise Russell

Imogen Stubbs has asserted her right to be identified as the author of
this work

Cover image by Dewynters; photography by John Rodgers

Typeset by Country Setting, Kingsdown, Kent CT14 8ES, UK
Printed and bound in Great Britain by CPI Antony Rowe, Chippenham,
Wiltshire

A CIP catalogue record for this book is available from the British Library

ISBN 978 1 85459 813 4

IMOGEN STUBBS

After reading English at Oxford, Imogen went to RADA.

Since then, she has acted in television, film and theatre, including time at the National Theatre and the RSC, in roles ranging from Desdemona, Viola, Gertrude and Saint Joan, to Ursula in *The Rainbow*, Sally Bowles in *Cabaret*, Anna in *Closer* and Stella in *A Streetcar Named Desire*.

She has written for many newspapers and magazines, and is co-writer of *Amazonian: Penguin Book of Women's New Travel Writing*. She has also co-written and directed the short film *Snow on Saturday*, which won the UCI Award for Best British Short.

We Happy Few is Imogen's first play. She has also workshopped a second play about Jeff Buckley and Eva Cassidy – which has fewer people and more songs.

For my mother Heather
who passionately believed one should be
brave enough to make a fool of oneself

Contents

Introduction

by Imogen Stubbs

Several years ago, my eye was caught by a photo in a newspaper of a group of women loading hampers into a Silver Ghost Rolls-Royce. A brief article explained that these seven women were the Osiris Players – a troupe of semi-strolling players led by a Miss Nancy Hewins who travelled across Britain taking theatre to people throughout the country who otherwise had no access to the arts at all. The photo was dated to the 1940s and although the Osiris company lasted for more than thirty years, the article focused on the war years. Between 1939 and 1945, these seven women had travelled tens of thousands of miles giving 1500 performances of a repertoire of over thirty-five plays. They travelled in various motor cars and when petrol was no longer available for private vehicles, by pioneer wagon and horse – and even by canoe. I thought their story would no doubt be snapped up as a wonderful idea for a road movie and forgot all about it.

And then I found myself in the Theatre Museum. My grandmother, Esther McCracken, was a well-known playwright during the 40s and 50s, having written two very popular comedies (*Quiet Weekend* and *Quiet Wedding*) and I was giving all the manuscripts I had inherited into the care of the Museum. While I was there, I remembered the Osiris Players and asked if, by any chance, the Museum had any record of them; they came back with five boxes of beautifully preserved archive. There were appointment books, programmes, photos, reviews, lighting plans – everything intact. And at the bottom was a never-published autobiography of the indomitable force behind the whole enterprise – Miss Nancy Hewins.

I found the experience of sifting through all this lovingly preserved information thrilling, funny and extremely moving. So I decided to write a play inspired by the Osiris story. I hasten to repeat 'inspired'. My play is a fiction; it is not in any way a documentary drama about 'Osiris' since many different women were involved over the years and their real stories were not to be reconciled with two or three hours' traffic of the stage. However, my impression was that Nancy – like Lilian Baylis – was a great pioneer in terms of theatre in education, and the notion of aspirational culture. It seems that from unpromising and often farcical beginnings, she developed a company that through 'blood, toil, tears and sweat' became a force to be reckoned with.

Like Blake, she thought of herself as an 'Awakener' – someone determined to stir people's faith in humanity in a time dominated by man's inhumanity to man.

Her chief weapons were a dogged determination, a courageous heart and, above all, Shakespeare. Her passion, and the passion she instilled in those around her, had a tremendous effect on thousands of young people.

Clearly, the themes of gender – women finding the resource to take over in a world suddenly vacated by men – and communality – the diversity that both separates and bonds a group of artists – were of immediate dramatic interest. But I suppose I respond to a nameless yearning for a lost age as well. Being in my forties, I feel myself suspended between two worlds: an 'old world' of telegrams, threepenny bits and Green Shield stamps and a 'new world' of computers and materialism. When I grew up, most people had lost fathers or grandfathers, uncles or cousins, in one or other of the Wars – and so my generation felt a direct, rather sombre responsibility to them for that sacrifice. But a sense of history seems at present to feel superfluous to many people, or even an encumbrance – as a teenager said to me recently, 'I hate history, it's so not now.' Our age seems to be sloughing off the burden of history, moving forward armed with incredible technology, but with an alarming lack of humility or identity. And as for the generation of my parents; those aliens from a bygone era of cottage hospitals and sock-darning and hymn-singing in Assembly ... of the days before the Union Jack was hijacked by the National Front or the makers of underpants for tourists, they seem to me in my cynical mood to have been consigned to a box labelled 'not relevant'.

I don't think we are the 'new race of philistines' that some fear, but we do live in a time when to be serious about a non-profit-making venture is looked on as madness – and our consumer society would have us believe that the Arts and spirituality have less to communicate than a mobile phone.

Nancy Hewins looked on the Arts as both our history and our heritage, and perhaps our horoscope too. She believed that through the power of storytelling, you could change society by touching people individually, harnessing the power of collective imagination. She believed that the point of life is 'connecting' – that the challenge of being a human being is about being 'we' not just 'me'. And that is also our gift.

She was lucky enough to witness the arrival in 1945 of the great reforming government of the last century – Attlee and Bevan. She was there for the creation of the most enlightened Welfare state, the National Health, the Arts Council, and the expansion of the BBC committed to the three Es.

Thanks to women, like Nancy, and not a few brave men too, I'd like to think I'm lucky to be here – a modern British woman. And what does that phrase really mean? I'm not sure; but I hope it means I have a beating heart and that I should try to carry on the same fight – for as Nancy, Euripides and my mother all had the habit of saying, 'Civilisation is not a gift of the Gods – it must be won anew by each generation.'

Acknowledgements

My great thanks to Nic Lloyd and Malvern Theatres, the Elmley Foundation, Carl Proctor, Hugh Wooldridge, Bill Kenwright, Thelma Holt and all the other astonishingly generous people who have helped launch the Artemis Players – but above all to Trevor Nunn and Serena Gordon, who have been the wind and the sails.

Special thanks also to David Threlfall, Stephen Rayne, Matthew Lloyd and Sandi Toksvig for their much valued input early on.

In Search of the Osiris Players
by Fred Moroni and Louise Russell

Those who go in search of the Osiris Players will no doubt
find themselves in an imposing building somewhere west of
Kensington. There they will find Blythe House, once the
London Post Office Savings Bank but now the home of the
London Theatre Museum Archive. And there, alongside
somewhat grander relics – early editions of Shakespeare
perhaps, or costumes worn by the great actors of the past –
they will find five dusty brown boxes which house almost all
that remains of the Osiris Repertory Company and whose
contents paint a broad, if somewhat incomplete tapestry of that
company throughout its thirty-odd years. There are posters and
playbills; receipts and account books; tour schedules and
lighting plots; letters and newspaper cuttings; but what
characterises this collection above all is the powerful presence
of the company's founder, Nancy Hewins, whose influence is
found on nearly every scrap of paper therein.

Born in Grosvenor Square in 1902, the last of three children and
the only girl, Nancy Hewins enjoyed a privileged childhood.
Her father, William Hewins was an economist and a friend of
the pioneering socialists Sidney and Beatrice Webb. They
appointed him to be the first director of the London School of
Economics. Beatrice Webb, who stood as godmother to Nancy,
described Hewins as 'original minded and full of energy and
faith', although she also noted his fanaticism, as did another
family friend: George Bernard Shaw. Hewins was later elected
to Parliament as the MP for Hereford and, at the height of his
career, became the Under Secretary of State for the colonies.

Nancy's background was thus no traditional one and it doubt-
less accounts for her radical streak, her social concern and her
sense of spiritual crusade. Unsurprisingly perhaps, she took a
degree in Philosophy, Politics and Economics, graduating from

St Hugh's College, Oxford, in 1924 with high honours. In his final report on Nancy, her tutor particularly praised her 'power of thought', and noted that her marks would have been still higher but for the fact that she suffered an episode of illness just prior to her exams.

Despite reading Politics, Nancy cherished no ambition to follow a career in that field and her first love seems to have been theatre from a relatively early age. As a teenager she made regular visits to the Old Vic where she was particularly inspired by the Benson Company's productions of *Henry IV* and *Henry V*. At university she became closely involved with amateur dramatics. Spurred on by her friend and mentor Sybil Thorndike, she was encouraged to found the so-called Isis Players once she finished her degree. Thorndike had said that 'it was no use trying to produce unless you could act' but at first Nancy did little acting, devoting herself instead to technical and administrative work. 'My real interest is in lighting effects, scenic design and the general management of the company,' she writes in her autobiography. Having learned carpentry and car mechanics from her brother and electronics from the family plumber, she was well equipped for the task. Indeed, the company's special lighting effects were to become particularly popular with audiences later on.

Isis was able to put on only one play a year, however, and Nancy soon became dispirited. It was then that she decided to put the company on a professional footing, re-naming it Osiris after Isis's husband and taking it on the road as a non-profit-making organisation. Nancy used her father's political contacts to secure support from the London County Council Education Office, who let the players rehearse in a disused school in Wandsworth. And in 1930, when a £40 donation from Lord Rothermere bought them mobility in the shape of an old Rolls-Royce (a second was bought soon after), as well as some much needed equipment, the company was able to give its first professional performance, to children at Oliver Goldsmith's School.

Around a year later, the company left London and toured productions of *Twelfth Night* and *Macbeth* to schools in Wallingford, a tour that secured them nearly 100 bookings from others around the country. Schools provided the company with a guaranteed audience and one that demanded an ever-wider repertory. *St Joan* (the play Shaw had written for Sybil Thorndike) was soon added to the existing list of Shakespeare and the classics. More Bernard Shaw plays followed. Then as war approached, it occurred to Nancy that the work of the Osiris Repertory Company might have still greater appeal. 'I suspected we might be useful with adults as well as children,' she wrote, adding that evacuation would swell the population in the countryside. Life would prove more difficult, however.

For one thing, petrol rationing meant that new means of transport would be required. The two Rolls-Royces, 'Mr Bumble' and 'Mrs Sowerberry', could no longer be kept on the road but a determined Nancy turned instead to horsepower. 'The horses were all right as far as they went,' she told the *Doncaster Gazette*. 'They revelled in being dressed in war trappings to take part in *Henry IV*, but they got rather up-stage about the less glamorous jobs.' It was after a particularly tiresome journey when Nancy claimed she nearly had to carry them on her back that she decided to put the horses into retirement. Again she made use of her family connections. Acknowledging the need for entertainment amid wartime austerity, the government labelled the players an essential service. From now on they were given a generous petrol allowance and were requested to play not only to schools but also in the villages themselves, performing to adults by night and children by day. The idea was to take theatre into areas, often remote, where otherwise there would be precious little.

It is not only in the big towns and cities that the English theatre flourishes – Parish halls and village greens provide the setting for the strolling players of today who are carrying on a centuries-old tradition that even war cannot stop. And in the quiet, rural districts, is found a genuine love of the theatre and an inherent appreciation of it that is all too often lacking in the more rarefied atmosphere of our theatres Royal. But those who tread the thespian way in such fashion have to live laborious days …Working on the communal system, the company makes it a rule never to refuse anyone, however inconvenient their facilities for

staging may be, or however small the village audiences.
To them the play is the thing in very truth.

Illustrated News, 29 May 1943

Life for an Osiris Player was extremely hard work. Sets and
stages varied from nothing at all, to castle ramparts, gardens
and even billiard tables, and were very often constructed
entirely from scratch by the girls on their arrival. Certainly it
can be said that no stage was ever easy. 'We were permanently
exhausted', ex-member Susan Date reminisced to *The
Independent*. And the word 'home' had very little meaning.
Even when not on tour, younger members of the company
found their lodgings in the so-called 'Barn', near Nancy's
house in Willersey, Worcestershire. 'Part of it was clear space
heated by a tortoise stove,' says Joanna Reid (nee MacLean),
an Osiris player from 1947-50. 'The other end,' she says, 'had
four cubicles, two down and two up reached by a ladder. They
were divided in the same way as a stage set with gas pipes and
curtains.' When on tour, the players often slept on the floors in
the school and village halls where they had performed. Barns,
cow houses, tents and caravans all played home too: 'we laid
our heads wherever we could,' remarked former Osirian Mary-
Rose Benton. This was everyday life for nearly forty years.

Members generally signed for a two-year period (with possible
'return visits' to help out in emergencies). They were encouraged
not to stay too much longer, for fear they might hinder their
chances of getting a 'real' acting part. The company's budget
allowed for seven players (including Nancy) at any given time.
They would be provided with food, shelter, clothing and
pocket money. 'If one of them needs a new winter coat, it isn't
a case of whether she can afford it personally, but whether the
company can. She always gets it', Nancy told the *Express and
Star* in 1951. Work was divided between the members and all
jobs relating to wardrobe, lighting, props and scenery were
skilfully undertaken. Members carried their own beds, cooked
their own meals, manoeuvred caravans and did their own
laundry where and however they could. It was a matter of what
was needed being done by whoever was willing. Nancy was
the only one without a 'practical' job to do. She had sole
responsibility for all the administration. It was a hard life but a

happy one, the *Manchester Evening News* reported, 'you only have to look at the tanned faces of these gypsy girls in their pullovers and slacks to realise that.'

Each member needed to show remarkable versatility and was often required to perform five or six parts in any one play. To keep the performance as smooth as possible, the players often 'underdressed', that is to say, they wore as many costumes as possible at any one time. Mary-Rose Benton gives an illuminating and detailed explanation of this process.

> In *Macbeth*, with nearly all my characters' clothes on at once, I began as a rather stout witch, changed to a less bulky Thane, slimmed down further into Banquo and, once the rubber dagger had been drawn across my throat, I became the Porter. After I had taken him off to answer the door, I took off his rough hessian, threw a gown on over my head, and glided back on as the Gentlewoman.

The touring schedule too was hectic and tiring. Performances were given at a rate of up to 250 a year, often with two or three in any given day. The company never turned down a request for a performance and the players soon became accustomed to long and varied journeys across the country. 'Strength is the operative word,' reported the *Doncaster Gazette*,

> Life as a strolling player needs that. There are the many chores to be dealt with that go with having a caravan home; the many jobs of rigging a stage, looking after lighting; packing up quickly for the journey to the next booking – all these require physical strength in addition to enthusiasm.

Facilities were inconvenient; audiences often small, yet there was no limit to the distances the Osiris Players would travel, often along poorly maintained roads in horrendous weather. A map of performances mirrors a dot-to-dot puzzle, ranging from Dornoch in Northeast Scotland to Guernsey in the Channel Islands. Specific tours of particular regions were also undertaken. In 1939, for instance, the company gave a series of perform-ances in the Rhondda Valley and a year later they toured Gloucestershire. The chief aim of the Osiris Players was to take the plays of Shakespeare and other dramatists within the reach of districts untouched by other companies. They

certainly succeeded. During the Second World War, a total
of 1500 performances were given, to children in daytime
and adults by night. And performances proved popular. The
company's account books for the period suggest an increase
from some fifty attendees per performance in 1931 to an
average of nearer one hundred by mid-1940. In fact, despite a
slight increase in both salaries and printing costs, the company
was able to pay off its overdraft at the end of 1941.

After the war, the players largely went back to touring schools,
although they did make annual trips to Guernsey, where they
formed part of a festival giving fourteen plays in as many nights.
By then, Nancy's house in Willersey had become a more perm-
anent base. Named 'The Long House', it is built of traditional
Cotswold stone and Nancy lived there with two other long-
standing members of the company: Constance Allen and Kay
Jones. Thus the company existed for a decade or more, until
1963 when it stopped travelling. For thirty-six years Nancy had
remained true to the founding values of the company: 'we
never refuse a request for a play.' In doing so, she had built
a repertoire of over fifty productions and had herself played
more than a hundred parts. Thereafter, theatre remained her
life. At first she took up a teaching post at the Birmingham
Theatre School and later was to set up a costume-hire business,
which ran throughout the 60s and into the 70s helping other
companies with lighting and staging. In 1977, shortly before
her death, Nancy looked back on fifty years of the Osiris
Players and her words are underpinned by a sense of crusade:

> Driving in an old black-and-white Rolls-Royce in Eire on a
> cold night with a wall of water over the windscreen, without
> knowing whether the car was on the road or in the river,
> crossing the Welsh mountains at two in the morning in snow
> and fog and finding the way by compass in wartime and
> even travelling with horses. These were some of the hazards
> normal to our life of taking plays of all kinds, from *Oedipus
> Rex* to Shakespeare, *Sweeney Todd* to *St Joan* and Noël
> Coward, whether in the Orkneys or the Channel Islands and
> Ireland with their stormy sea passages, or England, Scotland
> and Wales.

Less than a year later, Nancy died and was buried in St Peter's

Church near her home in Willersey, a quotation from *Cymbeline* on her grave.

> Fear no more the heat o'th'sun,
>   Nor the furious winter's rages;
> Thou thy worldly task hast done,
>   Home art gone and ta'en thy wages.

Act 4, Scene 2

She left The Long House to Wynne Griffiths, for two years an Osiris Player and something of a surrogate daughter to Nancy. Wynne Griffiths lives there still and the house is much as Nancy left it, her presence felt through a small portrait, drawn in sepia, which hangs in the hallway to this day.

Acknowledgements

The authors would like to thank former Osirians Barbara Baker, Mary Collins, Susan Date, Joanna Reid, Rosemary Hanbury-Brown and Mary-Rose Benton for their 'old days' stories. Also Patrick Hewins for the loan of his aunt's autobiography; Paul Barker, whose article in *The Independent* (4 June 1995) did much to revive interest in the Players; and the Society for Theatre Research for their funding of ongoing work on Nancy Hewins and the Osiris Repertory Company.

We Happy Few was first performed in London at the Gielgud Theatre on 29 June 2004 (previews from 17 June). The cast was as follows:

HETTY	Juliet Stevenson
FLORA	Marcia Warren
HELEN	Kate O'Mara
CHARLOTTE	Patsy Palmer
JOCELYN	Caroline Blakiston
REGGIE	Paul Bentley
GERTRUDE	Rosemary McHale
JOSEPH	Adam Davy
IVY	Cat Simmons
ROSALIND	Emma Darwall-Smith

Director Trevor Nunn
Designer John Napier
Costume Designer Elise Napier
Lighting Designer David Hersey
Choreographer Henry Metcalfe
Composer Steven Edis
Sound Designer Colin Pink

The play was performed in an earlier version at Malvern Theatres on 6 November 2003, directed by Stephen Rayne and designed by Soutra Gilmour.

WE HAPPY FEW

Imogen Stubbs

inspired by the Osiris Players

Characters

The Artemis Players
HETTY OAKS
FLORA PELMET
HELEN IRVING
ROSALIND ROBERTS
CHARLOTTE (CHARLIE) PETERS
JOCELYN THRIPP
IVY WILLIAMS
GERTRUDE ROSENBAUM
JOSEPH ROSENBAUM
REGGIE PELMET

Other characters can be played by members of the company, and include:

In the Wardrobe Store
LADY
MAN

The Ministry
LEONARD
MAUREEN

Auditionees
SHARON
ELSIE
HENRIETTA
WILLIAM

Others
KEITH
MAYOR
BERT

Assorted voices, announcers, newsreaders and characters, historical and literary.

ACT ONE

Darkness. Footsteps. A rim of light delineates a fastened double door at the very back of the space.

LADY'S VOICE. I think these are the keys . . .

A chain rattles and the first of several locks turns.

Don't hold your breath . . .

Two more locks turn.

MAN'S VOICE. We've probably found all we're gonna need from your main store, so maybe . . .

LADY'S VOICE. Fret not . . .

Another chain rattle and a final lock turn.

I've never been in here myself so I . . .

The doors creak open to reveal an ELDERLY LADY *carrying a torch, and a* YOUNG MAN.

LADY. Sesame! Here we are. 'Hetty's Horrors'.

She moves the torch-beam around to reveal an astonishing, cobwebbed souk of clothing and furniture, a mouldering wonderland of racks, rails (some two storeys high), criss-crossing lines of hanging garments like a back-street in Naples, mounds of chairs and tables, a throne, an upright piano, a stack of swords, a copse of lances, halberds and banners, a film projector, a small roll-top bureau, some tattered wings and a pram.

MAN. Jesus . . .

LADY. I rather agree. It must have felt like this when they opened Tutankhamen's tomb. What a cornucopia of . . . of . . . !

MAN. Of tat! What did you mean . . . Hetty's horrors?

LADY. Do you know I don't know and I should. I started here nearly fifteen years ago and they just used to call it 'Hetty's Horrors' . . . Ah lights lights! (*She finds a switch for a dim overhead bulb.*) Apparently she ran a company of some sort . . .

MAN. Oh right . . .

LADY. . . . and they toured about or something, and when they gave up, the whole caboodle, props, costumes, armoury was stored here. I think it was meant to be part of the hire store like all the other rooms, but I doubt if anyone has used this stuff in over fifty years.

The MAN *looks around, touches costumes hanging on rack, etc.*

MAN. No surprise there, then . . . It's the biggest pile of crap I've ever seen, . . . well, apart from everything nominated for the Oscars this year.

LADY. Overlooked were you?

MAN. What happened to cutting-edge? . . . It's all so yesterday . . . stick it in this mausoleum . . .

He switches on the projector. Nothing happens.

LADY. Anything take your fancy? Some lovely hessian.

MAN. What happened to these wings? . . . looks like dried-up ketchup or something . . . This place really spooks me . . . it's like being in Oxfam on acid.

LADY. Mmm. Though I'm afraid the nearest I've ever got to drugs was a Haliborange . . . It was just a thought. So which one are you thinking of doing Nineteen Forties?

MAN. *Titus Andronicus.*

LADY. Of course.

MAN. End of the war, end of an era . . . Shake it up a bit . . .

They move back to the door and she switches off the light.

LADY. I must see if there's an inventory for all this. God only knows what might be in here. Ah well . . . sorry to disturb . . . sleep . . . sleep . . .

She closes the doors and locks and chains are fastened again.

So what were you saying dear . . . one of the characters is a cross-dresser?

MAN. Saturninus, yeah, transsexual – not tutus . . . but fabulous as in ballroom dresses or anything with sequins.

A distant door slam. Darkness. Silence.

A VOICE. Bloody cheek! Give me strength!

From the costume rails:

ANOTHER VOICE (*whispered, amused*). Language. 'Hetty's Horrors'. You have to laugh . . . Hetty? (*Silence.*) *Hetty?*

HETTY. All those years of blood, toil, tears and sweat for what? 'So yesterday'? Since when were sequins 'cutting-edge'? Enough. You heard her. Sleep, Flora.

FLORA. Nil desperandum . . . we didn't do it to be remembered.

HETTY. 'Remember me.'

FLORA. 'Rest, rest, perturbed spirit.'

Silence.

The projector suddenly comes to life and throws an eerie image onto a dust sheet: a group of bearded men wearing cricket flannels clutching a Union Jack. The image changes to close-ups as the bearded faces laugh and hug and kiss each other. The film runs out and becomes numbers, etc. and then blank. The projector bulb goes out but the motor and spools continue to whir in the dark. Then all is silent.

I don't remember why we *did* do it.

HETTY. Oh for God's sake, Flora.

FLORA. There was the pageant, I remember that . . . but of course we were only there as Lights and Costume . . .

*A half-light, no more than an aura suffuses the nearest
racks of costumes, and stepping slowly and silently into the
space comes* QUEEN ELIZABETH I. *The faintest music
plays, the memory of 'Fantasia on a Theme by Thomas
Tallis' (Vaughan Williams), and* QUEEN VICTORIA,
*holding a prayer book, follows, her eyes cast down in
mourning. A spectral* BOUDICCA *glares ahead of her.*
ARTHUR *appears in armour, bearing Excalibur, as*
HETTY*'s voice is heard as if through a distant loudspeaker.*

HETTY. This royal throne of kings, this scept'red isle,
This earth of majesty, this seat of Mars,
This other Eden, demi-paradise . . .
This blessed plot, this earth, this realm, this England.
This land of such dear souls, this dear . . . dear God, where
the hell is Charles I? . . . Stop, stop, stop . . .

CHARLES I, *clean shaven, appears from behind* ARTHUR.

CHARLES I. Sorry, no beard as yet and no Derek either.

HETTY (*dressed in trench coat*). Flora, where's Charles I's
ruddy beard? And you little people – no, not you
Shakespeare, but Big Ben, Brittania and the Sopworth
Camel . . . yes, you . . . You are criss-crossing the pageant.
Kindly stick to the cross and cut the criss . . .

FLORA (*wearing slacks, sensible shoes and a headscarf*).
Sorry . . . My eyes are stinging from that spirit gum, ooh,
but then I do get hay fever every year so . . .

HETTY. I want a beard, Flora. Not your life story.

FLORA. Mea culpa, they've sent any number of Henry VIIIs
but not a Van Dyke in sight.

HETTY. Where the hell are the scissors? Honestly, Flora, do
I have to do everything myself . . . And where the hell's
Derek?

She strides away. FLORA *claps her hands.*

FLORA. Hello, sorry to be a wet blanket after that valiant
rehearsal but can I just say that when it comes to changing
into civvies, Tudors and Stuarts to the billiards room,
Angevins and Plantagenets to the ping-pong hut . . .

HETTY *returns cutting a beard out of something white.*

HETTY. Necessity is the mother of invention. That's what put the 'Great' into Britain.

She glues the make-shift beard on CHARLES I *rather brutally.*

CHARLES I. If you don't mind my saying, it seems a rather odd-looking beard . . .

HETTY. Not at all, you're quite right. It's a sanitary towel.

CHARLES I. A what?

FLORA. Kotex sanitary towel, dear . . . marvellous in a facial-hair crisis . . .

Everybody freezes except HETTY *and* FLORA.

Remember?

HETTY. No, I don't. But then I don't want to . . .

FLORA. How the director never turned up.

HETTY. Director? He couldn't direct Dorothy up the Yellow Brick Road.

FLORA. And you took over.

HETTY. Stood in.

FLORA. And you were doing so awfully well . . . Until the moment the wireless played over the loudspeakers . . .

CHAMBERLAIN'S VOICE, *echoing and fading from bad reception, comes as if from speakers, as the pageant cast huddle round.*

CHAMBERLAIN'S VOICE. 'This morning the British Ambassador in Berlin handed the German government a final note . . .'

HETTY. What I do remember was the Rosenbaums arriving from Germany – poor Gertrude and Joseph walking right into the middle of it . . .

A YOUNG MAN *and a* MIDDLE-AGED WOMAN *arrive in overcoats, carrying suitcases.*

CHAMBERLAIN'S VOICE. ' . . . their troops from Poland, a state of war would exist between us. I have to tell you that no such undertaking has been received and that consequently this country is at war with Germany . . .'

GERTRUDE (*quietly*). Herr Gott, Erbarme dich unser.

FLORA. What is she saying, dear?

JOSEPH. Please God, says she, on all of us be mercying.

HETTY. Quite right . . .

REGGIE. Hear, hear . . .

The radio plays the National Anthem. Everybody stands to attention. All take off hats and even wigs, and join in.

HETTY. I don't understand why we can't have 'Jerusalem'. Someone could at least try to write a National Anthem that's actually rousing. It really is a bloody awful tune.

FLORA. Worse for the poor Royals, of course . . . they can't get away from it . . . Oh mea multiply culpa, I should have introduced . . . Gertrude Rosenbaum and her son Joseph who are refugees who have come to us for safety from persecution in Germany . . . Welcome, both, at this sad moment for us all . . .

JOSEPH. Our thanks and thanks and ever thanks . . . Please forgiveness for the unspoken . . . my England is not very happy . . .

REGGIE (*who has been playing Charles I*). Nonsense and hello . . . I'm Reggie . . . Flora's cousin. You'll be staying with me and the gals if that's alright.

FLORA. I'm afraid that's me and Hetty – Miss Henrietta Oak . . .

HETTY. Guten Abend . . . [Good evening.]

REGGIE. Anyway, our home is your home. Speaking of which, I imagine everyone just wants to go now and be with their families . . .

FLORA. Yes, in the circumstances this all seems rather inappropriate. I fear we have no option but to abandon . . .

HETTY. Inappropriate? And let Hitler win before we've even started? 'In the circumstances', now is not the moment to become squeamish about patriotism. No, tonight . . . appropriately . . . our flame of resistance must shine out to remind us all that the spirit of our dear, dear land will never be extinguished. (*Applause begins.*) No! None of that! In the absence of your director, I shall take charge. And all I can say is that if the performance tonight is anything like that somnambulist exhibition at this rehearsal, I will personally garrotte myself. We have bath-water but we seem to have omitted baby. I want energy, clarity –

A siren is heard distantly over London, echoed by another.

FLORA. To the wine cellars.

REGGIE. Is that everyone or just the kings and queens?

Pandemonium as people rush for safety. The siren grows deafening and then suddenly stops. Everyone freeezes except HETTY *and* FLORA.

FLORA. That was the start of it, wasn't it? Yes?

HETTY. If only events had anything like that sort of order – Sudden patriotic fervour. I think not.

FLORA. What then? What?

HETTY. More like boredom . . . It was ages later . . . the recital.

FLORA. O my Lor' – Reggie's very beige front room in Kensington . . . so that Jocelyn could raise money for what? Refugees?

HETTY. Evacuees . . . Amputees . . . cream teas . . . God knows . . . she was never without a good cause . . . but that was when we first met the new 'maid' . . . our little bird . . .

IVY, *a girl of mixed-race origins with a very strong Midlands accent, is singing Billie Holiday-style as she billows a white tablecloth.* REGGIE *appears with an elderly eccentric,* JOCELYN THRIPP.

REGGIE. Ivy, could you clear away the tea?

IVY. Is that wise, Mister Pelmet? I really wouldn't trust me with fancy foreign crockery.

FLORA. And Jocelyn requested silence for her 'practice warble'.

REGGIE. Good God, are *you* going to be singing, Miss Thripp?

JOCELYN. I always like to finish my charity evenings with 'Only God Can Make a Tree'. Seems to send people rushing for the buckets . . .

JOSEPH *goes to help* IVY *who is struggling with the tray.*

JOSEPH (*gently*). 'Who would fardles bear?'

IVY. Sorroy . . . ?

JOSEPH. 'To grunt and sweat under a weary life.' Hamlet . . .

IVY. Oh right . . . nice to meet you, Hamlet. I'm Ivy . . .

REGGIE. Oh for heaven's sake, Ivy, get on with it . . .

IVY *exits with the tray. As she disappears out of sight, there is a crash, 'Oh bloody bogger it . . .'* IVY *leans her head back round the door.*

IVY. Sorroy!

FLORA. And the Rosenbaums played.

GERTRUDE *is playing the slow movement of Brahms' First Piano Concerto.*

Gertrude made us weep with her Mendelssohn and Schubert and Brahms – all Germans – peering into the very soul of humankind.

The music swells, becoming JOSEPH *playing the saxophone. The clothing rails move slowly, turning on their axes but clearing a much bigger central space, and revealing chairs and a few tailors' dummies costumed appropriately for late 1930s smart.*

HETTY. And Joseph played Gershwin – hands across the sea . . .

Applause gives way to the sound of chatter as the impression of a post-performance party is created in the half-light . . .

JOCELYN. What a very remarkable young man.

FLORA. In every way. Joseph's father taught him English by reading him all the plays of Shakespeare and that's why his English is so terribly . . . unusual . . . and rather touching somehow . . .

JOCELYN. I thought all refugees were being sent to the Isle of Man.

FLORA takes a sandwich from IVY *as* JOCELYN *moves off.*

FLORA. Yes, well the Rosenbaums will have to face a tribunal, and the policy seems to pack off anyone who's German, even if they are Jewish – unless they're gainfully employed I suppose . . . ooh Ivy . . . Sandwich spread and pilchard?

IVY. Do you like it?

FLORA. It's an acquired taste . . .

HETTY. It's utterly ridiculous, Flora. You and I should be doing something.

FLORA. Do you mean like a duet? I can't sing for toffee.

HETTY. Not tonight, you dolt. I mean something a great deal more ambitious than 'Only God Can Make a Tree'. We have skills. We should be gainfully employing them.

JOCELYN *approaches again.*

JOCELYN. I'm afraid according to *The Times* yesterday, the official war-term for housewives is now 'The unoccupied classes.'

HETTY. Give me strength . . .

HETTY *moves away.* JOCELYN *turns to* JOSEPH.

JOCELYN. Are you enjoying London? Have you been doing something jolly?

JOSEPH. I have been making a sight-see and have laid waste to time . . .

JOCELYN. Oh dear . . .

JOSEPH. . . . but today I am putting money in my purse to give to our kind hosts for our food and so forth . . .

FLORA *is circulating.*

FLORA. Not at all . . .

JOSEPH. Yes, forthwith! I have a job with a big band for swinging.

JOCELYN. Swinging what?

IVY (*with a drinks tray*). You mean a swing band?

JOSEPH. Yes yes, you are hitting the eye of the bull.

JOCELYN. Bull's eye.

JOSEPH. Bottom up! (*He takes a drink.*)

LEONARD, *a man in a bad toupee, cuts in.*

LEONARD. Hey Cocoa – Cocoa! Give me one of those would you?

GERTRUDE (*takes* JOSEPH *aside*). Hast du ihnen von deinem Auftrag erzählt? [Did you tell them about your job?]

JOSEPH. Ja, aber ich glaube nicht dass sie mich verstanden haben. [I did but I don't think they understood.]

LEONARD (*confiding in* HETTY). Damned uncomfortable being entertained by the Hun. Can't abide their language . . . or their music come to that . . .

HETTY. These people are refugees who . . .

LEONARD. No, honestly, as I was saying, this war's made women so damn bored and restless. I don't know – Avril's helping with some 'Health through Housework' campaign What sort of tommyrot's that? 'Healthy Buttocks against Hitler'? (*He roars with laughter.*)

HETTY. The girl's name is Ivy not Cocoa and who knows . . . if this war goes on then perhaps she'll be stepping into your job one day . . .

LEONARD. Just like the last war . . . a woman's place is to keep the home fires burning.

HETTY. And who's going to do the men's jobs when they all get called up?

LEONARD. So which one of the men's jobs are you after 'matey'? I s'pose you want to be a lumberjack . . . (*He laughs.*)

HETTY. Well, actually, I'm so 'damn bored and restless', I'm putting together an acting company to take Shakespeare to people throughout Britain who, now that the theatres are dark, have no access to our great culture whatsoever . . .

FLORA *looks astonished.*

LEONARD. Ah! That's different! Taking sweetness and light to the raw unkindled masses. 'To be or not to be, that is the question'? And this is the answer – 'Bugger off!'

He roars with laughter. There is a crash. IVY *comes forward.*

IVY. Excuse me, Miss Pelmet, would you mind if I asked you a personal question?

FLORA. What is it?

IVY. How incredibly fond would you say Mister Pelmet was of that little teapot with the green monsters on it?

FLORA. The Wedgwood dragon?

IVY. That's the one . . .

FLORA. Incredibly.

IVY. Righto . . .

IVY *disappears.*

LEONARD. Well . . . the little woman will be wondering where I've got to . . .

HETTY. Tell me . . . do you act yourself?

LEONARD. Do I look like a Nancy-boy?

HETTY. I'm so sorry, I just assumed that's why you were
wearing that appalling wig . . .

LEONARD. I think I'd better go . . .

He starts to leave.

HETTY. I think you better had . . . before you disappear up
your capacious arse into the unchartered regions of your
own inadequacy . . . matey.

LEONARD *exits furiously.*

FLORA. Hetty!

HETTY. What?

FLORA. Oh Hetty . . . how brave . . .

HETTY. You and I could be making a real contribution.

FLORA. You mean you're serious about a theatre company?
But all the men will be busy . . .

HETTY. Then we'll just have to use the 'unoccupied' classes.

FLORA. Only women?

HETTY. Why not? I'm damned if I'm going to spend this war
making chutney and knitting pom-pom hats.

JOCELYN *sings the last line of 'Only God Can Make a Tree'.*

Everyone freezes except HETTY *and* FLORA.

That was when it started . . . yes?

FLORA. I don't think I took you seriously even then . . .

IVY *unfreezes.*

IVY. Sorroy to butt in . . . but it's actually quite funny, you see,
because that wasn't the only thing that started that day . . .
Everyone had gone home and I was clearing up . . .

The wireless is playing a song. IVY *is singing along as she
clears up. She gets carried away and performs the end of
the song full out.* JOSEPH *appears and touches her
shoulder enthusiastically.*

JOSEPH. If I profane with my unworthy hand . . .

IVY. How very embarrassing.

JOSEPH. Not at all. You are singing smeshing well. May I propose to you?

IVY. Oh yeah, very funny . . .

JOSEPH. No . . . may I propose a clement idea to make a sing-song with me?

IVY. I just have to make a snack for Mister Pelmet.

JOSEPH. Sneck?

IVY. Make omelette . . . Omelette.

JOSEPH. No, Joseph . . . I am Joseph.

IVY. Oh bloody bogger . . . we're going round in circles.

JOSEPH. Sorroy for my bad language . . . you must please with my band to be singing, yes? . . .

She laughs. He picks up the sax and starts to play. She scats and swirls around. As she does so, one of the double storey racks turns around to reveal a white wall on the other side. A stack of letters swirls into the air like a flock of deranged seagulls. HETTY *gathers them together tenderly and reads.*

HETTY (*reads*). 'My darling Crispian, I wake up every day hoping for some news of you, my love. I worry and I miss you so much, my darling, it's wretched. Enough gloom and despond . . . I'm still living with my friend Flora in London which is safe enough at present, but we're so bored we are starting an all-women Shakespeare company – there I knew I would make you laugh – '

FLORA (*on phone*). 'Shakespeare with a difference. Full Stop. The formation of a classical ensemble. Stop. Saturday 2nd December. The Sir William Poole room – Pimlico Junior School. Stop. Have prepared a speech by any of the Bard's male characters. Exclamation mark. Ladies only. Full stop. Amateurs welcome.'

HETTY (*reads*). 'However, we're just at the audition stage so with any luck it will all fall through . . . '

Music. HETTY, GERTRUDE, FLORA *arrive at a school porter's desk. A young tomboy,* CHARLIE, *is on the phone.*

FLORA. Excuse me, young man . . . We have booked a room here this afternoon . . . I take it you're the holiday schoolporter . . .

CHARLIE. Dunno a thing about it, mate . . . (*Back on the phone.*) I've got one for the three o'clock . . . (*She looks at her newspaper.*) Euridice. (*Pronounced 'You're a dice'.*)

FLORA. Sorry, I'm absolutely feeble with names, but I think it's 'Euridisee'.

CHARLIE. Don't you get smart with me . . . Standin' there like Freeman Hardy and Willis . . . yeah, put a bob each way on 'Euridice'.

FLORA *hands* CHARLIE *a letter.*

FLORA. You are instructed to bring the ladies on this list to us, as and when they arrive . . . Would you then announce their names and what part they are playing. We shall be in the room named, I believe, after the illustrious Sir William Poole . . . (*To* HETTY.) which apparently is a large space with thrilling acoustics . . .

There is a pause.

HETTY. Well – how do we get there?

CHARLIE. Across there – down the corridor, big doors on the right . . . can't miss it. (*They set off.*) And it's pronounced 'Swimming Pool'.

They turn back in horror.

FLORA. Mea entirely culpa.

HETTY. Ruddy hell, Flora . . . the Marx Brothers could organise things better . . . We'll just have to see if we can make do with a classroom.

Music.

FLORA *and* HETTY *stand beside tiny chairs in a primary school classroom.* GERTRUDE *tries out the piano.*

GERTRUDE. Das Klavier muss gestimmt werden ... das 'mittlere C' ist kaputt. [This piano needs tuning . . . the 'middle C' is kaput.]

CHARLIE appears, whistling a little tune.

CHARLIE. The first lamb to the slaughter is standing by . . . I'm Charlie by the way . . . (*Announcing.*) Miss Sharon Poulette.

SHARON (*as she enters*). 'Poulet' the 'et' is pronounced 'ay' as in the French chicken . . .

CHARLIE. Miss Sharon Poulay with a speech from *Hamlay* as in the French pig . . .

As she begins . . . Blackout.

Music plays between each audition like musical chairs.

Another girl enters. She hands GERTRUDE some sheet music.

CHARLIE. Miss Elsie Carter, doin' the 'Seven Ages' as Jacks from *As You Like It.*

ELSIE. Two, three . . . four –

From the word go, she tap dances around the dialogue and then exits . . . and re-enters.

'All . . . the world's a stage . . .
And all . . . the men and women merely players;
They have their exits . . . (*Exits.*) . . .
(*Re-enters.*) and their entrances' . . .

The women look aghast.

HETTY. Thank you. Are you, by any chance, a fan of Mister Fred Astaire?

ELSIE. How did you guess?

FLORA. We're all fascinated to know what . . . inspired you to play Jacques as a tap dancer?

ELSIE. Well, your advertisement said 'Shakespeare with a difference'.

HETTY *looks ill. Music.*

CHARLIE. Miss Henrietta Trend as Titus Andronicus –

HENRIETTA. I brought my own pie . . .

Music.

CHARLIE. Next we have Mrs Evelyn Unpronounceable and . . .
Anyway, she's going to be doing Richard one hundred and
eleven.

HETTY. Flora. Tea.

Music. A man appears with CHARLIE.

CHARLIE. William Beadle will do Pericles. (*Pronounced
'Bicycles'.*)

WILLIAM. Pericl*ee*s.

HETTY. You're a man.

WILLIAM. D'you have a problem with that?

HETTY. Yes. Next . . .

CHARLIE. I think that might be it, 'cos there ain't no one else
waitin'.

CHARLIE *exits, passing* FLORA *entering with a jug of
water and glasses.* GERTRUDE *plays a Chopin nocturne.*

FLORA. Wouldn't a man be useful? I mean actually Gertrude's
Joseph would be perfect . . .

HETTY. Absolutely not . . . he'd make women playing men
look silly and throw a colossal spanner in the sleeping
arrangements . . .

FLORA. Of course . . . oh I forgot to tell you . . . I've
persuaded Reggie to lend us his old car for our transport . . .
Well, it's been mouldering in his garage for years . . . He
even gave me this photograph of it . . . in case it might serve
as an inducement to ditherers.

Music continues. CHARLIE *brings in* ROSALIND
ROBERTS *fully-costumed as Shylock: skullcap, long-hair*

*coat and a false nose. She begins in dumb show but as the
music fades . . .*

ROSALIND. ' . . . cooled my friends, heated mine enemies.
And what's his reason? I am a Jew. Hath not a Jew eyes?
Hath not a Jew hands, organs, dimensions, senses, passions .
. . Fed with . . . '

HETTY *calls her over.* ROSALIND *is very nervous.*

HETTY. Thank you, Miss Roberts. Now Rosalind, talking of
organs, Mrs Rosenbaum here is Jewish but look! Her nose
is quite normal . . . as I'm sure yours is underneath that
putty . . .

ROSALIND. Oh gosh, I'm so sorry. I thought some disguise
might be required and anyway, they always did it like that
when Mummy was at the Old Vic. And the truth is . . . I hate
my own nose . . .

HETTY. So you've just left the RADA, Rosalind?

ROSALIND. Yes, but I am quite used to playing chaps because
I went to a convent you see . . . actually, I got the award for
stage fighting.

FLORA. Oh! I once got an awfully sweet award for knitting all
the chain mail for *Saint Joan.*

HETTY. Flora, do stop trying to sound like a woman with an
interesting past . . . And you have no dependants – dogs,
children, that sort of thing?

ROSALIND. Oh no . . . well – only Mummy.

HETTY. Good – you look like a girl with an adventurous
spirit. We'll be in touch.

ROSALIND. Oh please don't think you have to . . . Anyway,
thanks awfully for seeing me . . . I wasn't sure you would
because of your advertisement.

HETTY. The advertisement?

ROSALIND (*bringing out a bit of newspaper*). Yes, look, it
says, 'Ladies. Full Stop. Only amateurs welcome.'

FLORA. Mea typographically culpa.

ROSALIND. Anyway, I'm frightfully sorry about the nose
fiasco . . . Verzeihe mir, Frau Rosenbaum [Forgive me.]. . .
and best of luck with everything . . .

ROSALIND *leaves.* GERTRUDE *begins trying to tune a
note on the piano.*

HETTY. Now, we've got four bearables – this last one . . . and
those three who'd just left the Central School were
serviceable . . .

FLORA. What about the King Lear? . . . you know . . . the one
in the rather vivacious rain-bonnet?

HETTY. If they are to play different characters none of the girls
can be too distinctive, yes? That Lear had Brobdingnagian
breasts . . .

FLORA. I suppose we're rather on the lookout for Lilliputian
breasts, aren't we?

GERTRUDE *is whacking a note on the piano.*

HETTY. Well, let's hope – (*Shouts.*) We can live without
'middle C', thank you, Gertrude . . .

FLORA. She's in a bit of a tizz, about the tribunal being
postponed yet again . . . Anyway, well done us for getting
this far . . .

HETTY. Not exactly the Moscow Art as yet, is it?

CHARLIE *pops her head round the door.*

CHARLIE. There's a late arrival . . . Miss Charlotte Peters.
(*She goes off. And comes in again, taking her cap off.*)
It's me . . . but I've gone right off the idea . . . I'm goin'
home . . .

HETTY. Absolutely not . . .

FLORA. Take heart, dear, you can't possibly be worse than
Miss Edith Rutter and her indescribably vulgar
interpretation of 'Blow, wind, and crack your cheeks'.

CHARLIE. I 'aven't got a speech and you've 'eard me whistle
so I can do a joke or a magic trick . . .

HETTY *is looking through a pile of typed sheets.*

HETTY. We'll have the magic trick, thank you.

    CHARLIE *comes forward, she picks up the glass and the jug, pours water into the jug.*

CHARLIE. Jug water – water jug. (*She tips the jug slowly over* FLORA*'s head.*)

    Alakazam! (*No water comes out.*)

HETTY. Bravo . . . Now I want you to read this . . .

She hands her a typewritten page.

CHARLIE. I'm diabolical at reading . . .

HETTY. Diabolical's fine, just have a go . . .

    CHARLIE *reads the speech, haltingly mispronouncing words, and almost comically.*

CHARLIE. Henry Vee. 'O . . . God of battles steel my soldiers' . . . hearts possess them not . . . with fear take from them now the sense . . . of reckoning if the oppos'd . . . ' I can't –

HETTY. Oppos*è*d . . . Good, that's right . . . Always follow the thought through to the end . . . and just imagine . . . this young man . . . this king . . . he has these soldiers' lives in his hands and he's only the same age as you . . . 'take from them now the sense of reckoning' – counting, adding up, y'see, he's praying his soldiers won't work out how terribly outnumbered they are . . . He's praying for courage . . . well, I think in our own way we've all been there, haven't we, Charlie? Have another go . . . and just say it to me . . . don't worry about anyone else . . .

    CHARLIE *improves and somehow becomes very moving.*

CHARLIE. 'O God of battles! Steel my soldiers' hearts;
Possess them not with fear; take from them now
The sense of reckoning, lest the opposed numbers
Pluck their hearts from them. Not today, O Lord!
O not today . . . '

She gets tearful and stops. The water that magically disappeared pours out of the jug and splashes on the floor (these magic jugs are available from Davenport's Magic Shop, Charing Cross, London).

HETTY. Can you cook?

CHARLIE *shakes her head sadly.*

FLORA. Can you sew?

CHARLIE *sniffs and shakes her head.*

HETTY. Can you change a tyre?

CHARLIE*'s face lights up.*

CHARLIE. Yes Yes! I bloody can. My brother Tommy's a mechanic . . . only he's just been called up . . .

HETTY. So what can you tell us about *our* transport . . . ?

She hands her the photograph.

CHARLIE. Silver Ghost Rolls-Royce 1922 – only the bloody Shakespeare of the road!

They all laugh.

CHARLIE. Am I in?

HETTY. Yes, I think you are.

CHARLIE. Bloody Nora!

HETTY. Well . . . notionally.

CHARLIE. Come again?

FLORA. We haven't actually got Ministry permission . . . as yet.

CHARLIE. Well, you'll be alright . . . you're posh enough, in't yer? Odds on . . .

HETTY. I wouldn't bet on it.

MAUREEN, *a lady official, leads* HETTY *and* FLORA *along corridors to a gloomy Home Office room.*

MAUREEN. So. If there is to be conscription of women you're wanting 'Reserved occupation' status for your troupe of 'players'.

HETTY. All we require is a petrol ration for one, possibly two vehicles; itinerant status for the troupe vis-à-vis food vouchers, etc. and a small advance for set, props and costumes. Salaries will be negligible, it will be a co-operative.

MAUREEN. And this is to be your contribution to the War effort? I take it this is to be a non-profit-making venture.

HETTY. I can say with the absolute certainty that comes from a lifetime involved with the theatre that it will be making no profit whatsoever.

MAUREEN. Ah, here's the minister.

A man appears. It is LEONARD *of the toupee.*

FLORA. Oh Lor', it can't be . . .

LEONARD. Do sit down. I believe we've already discussed the aforementioned proposition, and so you know I'm at a loss to understand why we should consider the performance of Shakespeare and his *ilk* of this order of resource-priority when we are at war? We have to deal with more practical considerations . . . A little group of Thespia will hardly serve as a deterrent to the Germans . . .

HETTY. Of course not . . .

FLORA. People . . . children especially . . . need stories to cheer them up . . . to distract them from all the . . . the . . .

HETTY. We have schools to nurture the mind, food to nurture the body but where do we look to nurture the soul?

LEONARD. To religion surely.

HETTY. Religion? That's usually the cause of men going to war in the first place . . . no, I mean to the Arts.

LEONARD. This war has nothing to do with religion . . . We're fighting against a ruthless dictatorship.

HETTY. Yes but what are we fighting *for*? What is there about Britain we hold dear enough to die for? The land that gave the world Shakespeare . . . There wasn't an English language till he made it . . . he taught us how to think . . .

to understand how complicated we can allow ourselves to be . . . to see . . .

LEONARD. . . . 'into the unchartered regions of our own inadequacy'? I remain unconvinced that storytellers can lay claim to any of our meagre resources nor can they be deemed essential to children in our current climate . . .

HETTY. Not essential to children . . . storytellers?

LEONARD. We must get on . . . thank you . . .

FLORA. Thank you for your time.

HETTY and FLORA go to leave. As she is leaving, HETTY turns.

HETTY. I knew a child . . . he was sick . . . he was very sick with TB . . . bless him but . . . Anyway, I went to visit him one day and he had his hands cupped like this . . . and when I reached him he opened them and a butterfly flew out and up up into the air . . . around and around . . . and he was so happy . . . and then the butterfly dropped from . . . it just dropped . . . and his little face crumpled up . . . I mean he was overwhelmed with grief . . . at life's unfair transience . . . and he picked it up so gently and he whispered . . . and he really did say this . . . 'Goodnight, sweet prince, and flights of angels sing thee to thy rest . . .'

Silence. MAUREEN blows her nose tearfully.

He's back in hospital now but you see that's what all of us want . . . those moments of inspiration when language is lit up by life . . . or life by language . . .

LEONARD. Wait here a moment. Maureen.

LEONARD and MAUREEN exit.

HETTY. Remind me next time I do that story to come up with a more plausible quote . . .

LEONARD returns.

LEONARD. Very well. I'm going to put you on trial.

FLORA. Oh but . . .

LEONARD. One play, four weeks to get it organised, strict budget limitation. Now let's see, the play I want you to tackle . . . ah yes . . . yes, that should sort things out . . . *Macbeth*.

LEONARD *exits.*

There is an incredible saxophone riff.

FLORA. Come on . . . I want to take you somewhere . . . to celebrate!

A crazy high-energy dance floor. JOSEPH on saxophone.
A glamorous girl stands next to JOSEPH and starts to sing.
It's IVY – in her element. HETTY and FLORA are there.
As the song hits a saxophone break, everyone freezes except
IVY who joins HETTY and FLORA.

IVY. Oh my God, it was so thrilling. I'd never felt so . . . special before . . .

HETTY. You were transformed . . . shimmering . . .

FLORA. Billie Holiday meets Josephine Baker.

HETTY. Transformed.

IVY. Oh bloody bogger! It's me again . . .

She rushes back to finish the last verse of the song. The
music swells as another double-height rail swirls around to
make a stark white space.

HETTY meets her assembled company. Behind her is a
costume rail crammed with clothes from different shows.
In front of her is a table on which a model theatre is hidden
under a scarf and some props. There is a film-projector.
FLORA stands beside her. It is something of a double-act.

HETTY. I am Miss Oak, I am light; Mrs Pelmet is costume; Mrs Rosenbaum is music, and Mister Rosenbaum is stage management. The rest of you are prop men, prompters, ticket-sellers, treasurers, armourers, carpenters, cooks, car mechanics, and eventually kings, Gods and a host of fascinating people.

FLORA. We shall be known as The Artemis Players after the Goddess Artemis – spreader of sunlight and the creative spirit and also protector of children . . . To begin with we will play only forty characters between the seven of us . . .

HETTY. But if we meet with success, then in time we seven will carry within us several hundred characters. We shall live a circus life, the life of gypsies – sleeping on God knows what, God knows where – performing in primary schools, church halls, village greens . . . munitions factories . . .

FLORA. We will transport our own stage which we must be able to put up and take down ourselves in under an hour . . .

HETTY. As to decor . . . uncluttered and simple – I'm not in favour of design where the actors lower the tone of the set . . .

FLORA. Then for Wardrobe – you will learn that a little paint and some hessian can clothe a beggar or an army or a king . . . and this little 'aide de combat' – (*She reveals a corset-like object.*) – will help camouflage those extraneous breasts –

HETTY. We shall learn to fight . . . (*She lunges at an unsuspecting* FLORA.) . . . for which, Flora, we must be fit and alert . . .

FLORA. And we will learn to dance.

HETTY. We must master the accents of every region in Britain – for when it comes to differentiating characters there is no greater ally than the regional accent . . . (*With a Cockney accent.*) 'His nose was as sharp as a pen and a' babbled of green fields.'

Pause.

FLORA. Cockney . . . Ooh is it my go? (*With her attempt at a Welsh accent.*) 'I will make him eat some of my leek or I will beat his pate four days . . .'

HETTY. Um . . .

FLORA. That's right, Welsh . . . and so on.

HETTY. Now let's get this out of the way once and for all . . .
Kissing . . . settle down . . . there's nothing to snigger at . . .
it's a perfectly natural thing . . . However, to adapt to our
particular situation requires a simple sleight of hand . . .
Flora. All of you, try it.

They kiss their own thumbs next to each other's lips.

FLORA. You three . . . yes, the gigglers from Central . . .
you're being very silly girls . . .

HETTY. As women, we can play all the heroines . . . Flora.

FLORA (*demonstrates*). 'Gallop apace, you fiery-footed
steeds, towards Phoebus' lodging . . . '

HETTY. And we can play the girl pretending to be a boy . . .
Flora.

FLORA (*demonstrates*). 'My father had a daughter loved a
man, as it might be perhaps, were I a woman, I should your
lordship . . .'

HETTY. But our great task will be to play the men . . . to find
the man inside each and every one of us – his voice, his
gestures, his expressions . . . Flora.

FLORA (*demonstrates*). 'Once more unto the breach, dear
friends, once more; Or close the wall up with our English
dead . . . '

There is a smattering of applause which FLORA *accepts
graciously.*

HETTY. No . . . no, none of that . . . no need for that. We must
scrutinise men . . . faces, faces . . . here are male faces . . .

She switches on the projector as FLORA *switches off the
lights. Footage appears of Hitler, Stalin, Winston Churchill,
Errol Flynn, etc.*

What intrinsically makes a man different from a woman?
Centuries of our acceptance that they have the power, the
status, the authority?

FLORA. Their desire to fight, to possess, to destroy – where a
woman's instinct might be to negotiate, protect, create?

HETTY. Or are men moulded by the women around them –
their adoring mothers, their subservient wives . . . or in the
case of Mister Errol Flynn . . .

Everyone goes 'Oooh!'

Exactly . . . the hysterical female response to a meagre
moustache and a tight pair of breeches . . .

FLORA. We shall be grappling with thirty-five of the greatest
works of the last four hundred years . . . Sophocles to
Winnie the Pooh . . .

HETTY. But to achieve all this we must begin by grappling
only one, *Macbeth* . . . It is a timely play – a play about the
thrilling ascendancy of evil and the halting retaliations of
the good . . . We have just one month to prove to the
Ministry that we're worth their money and every hope that
our first performance will be given in the legendary Hoxton
Hall . . . which very fittingly is a place renowned as a home
for theatrical innovation . . . Now this might be a good
moment for me to call a break.

Everyone freezes. Except ROSALIND *and* CHARLIE.

CHARLIE. But you didn't – worst luck – you got us doing
some sort of poxy game thing . . . to show us just how much
we'd have to rely on each other.

ROSALIND. 'Take a line each of this speech . . .

CHARLIE. . . . and like a relay-runner pass the baton to your
team-mate – pass on the thought . . .

ROSALIND *and* CHARLIE. . . . You won't achieve anything
that sounds remotely human to begin with . . .'

The scene returns to the past.

HETTY (*hands out papers*). . . . but we shall persist and in the
end we shall seem to be one voice, thinking with one mind,
feeling with one heart . . .

'Tomorrow . . . and tomorrow and tomorrow . . .

FLORA. . . . Creeps in this petty pace from day to day . . .

ROSALIND. To the last syllable of recorded time . . .

CHARLIE. And all our yesterdays have lighted fools . . .

VOICE 1. The way to dusty death . . . Out, out, brief candle.

VOICE 2. Life's but a walking shadow, a poor player . . .

VOICE 3. That struts and frets his hour upon the stage . . .

> IVY *and* JOSEPH *are walking in the dark under an umbrella. They have a torch.* JOSEPH *is reading out the typed sheet of 'Tomorrow . . .'*

JOSEPH. And then is heard no more; it is a tale
Told by an idiot, full of sound and fury . . .

IVY. . . . signifying nothing . . .'

> Bloody bogger it. Is that what Shakespeare's like? It's incredibly depressing . . .

JOSEPH. No no, Ivy . . . His language . . . it is his swing music and his blues . . . O that I were a glove upon that hand . . .

He takes her hand.

IVY. Shurrup, you daft plonker . . . Anyway, your mum would be none too happy about that . . . Hey, what does it say on the bench, Joe? . . . Switch the torch on a minute . . .

JOSEPH. 'Jim and Elsie always and forever . . .

IVY. . . . 1914.' I wonder if they made it through . . .

They sit down.

JOSEPH. So what is the story of Ivy?

IVY. There's nothing to say really . . . I've always been in domestic service even though I'm rubbish at it. Sometimes I say my dad's Paul Robeson but I've never had a family, like a mum or anything . . . I was brought up in an orphanage . . . you know Doctor Barnado's Home?

JOSEPH. Oh . . . Has he been away?

IVY. So what about your dad?

JOSEPH. My father, he is doctor . . . his especial job is bring babies into this world . . . Jewish babies, Christian babies . . . he is not judging . . .

IVY. Why didn't he come to England with you?

JOSEPH. Kristallnacht – the night of broken glass – there is much violent against the Jewish people . . . a woman is coming to our house with a baby in her arms . . . its little body so bloody and she is begging, 'Lass mein Baby nicht sterben' . . . 'Don't let my baby die' . . . My father is holding baby in his arms as it is screaming. My mother has only hatred for those who are doing this . . . my father has only love for those who are suffering . . . So no . . . no . . . he is not for leaving . . .

They hold hands under the umbrella in silence. An ARP WARDEN *shouts 'Put that light out.'*

HETTY *reads another letter at the bureau.*

HETTY (*reads*). 'My own dear Crispian. My darling, you are the only person I can tell how sick I feel before every rehearsal – a combination of adrenalin and animal fear . . . I have to sit on the floor of the bathroom and talk myself into getting to my feet and going to confront all those expectant faces . . . It must be something like this going into battle . . . dear God, how shameful of me to compare the two . . . '

ROSALIND *and* CHARLIE *cross the stage fighting to Gracie Fields' 'Sing as You Go'.*

ROSALIND. Left right, left right, spin and lunge . . . Ouch! You clumsy oik! Come on, we've only got ten more days, you're supposed to have learned it by now.

CHARLIE. Keep your hair on, Douglas Fairbanks . . . We ain't got Hoxton Hall and we ain't gonna make that deadline so it's all a waste of bloody time . . . I'm gonna get myself a nice cuppa char . . .

ROSALIND. Oh right . . . that's marvellous . . . So if we do get a venue, I'm supposed to look a ninny in the fights just because you want to slob about drinking nice cuppas of char.

ROSALIND *leaves as* IVY *and* REGGIE *arrive. They are carrying tea things.*

IVY. If you were ever a Hollywood star, what would you call yourself?

REGGIE. Gosh . . . I don't know . . . Victor Immature . . . or maybe Larry Panache . . .

IVY. I'd call myself Bliss . . . Bliss Williams . . . that'd be nice. Mister Pelmet, with all this Shakespeare stuff going on, can I ask you something that's bin worryin' me?

REGGIE. Fire away, Miss Williams . . . or can I call you Bliss?

IVY. In the olden days – like, say, the actors in Shakespeare an' all that – well, what did they use for toilet paper?

REGGIE. Well . . . books and scripts were written on very thin paper – so once they'd learned their parts – Romeo, Julius Caesar, whatever . . . the actors . . .

IVY. Really?

REGGIE. Absolutely.

IVY. I've never seen a Shakespeare play – What're they like?

REGGIE. Long . . .

IVY. Oh right . . .

REGGIE. Lots of yattering – shouting – that sort of thing . . .

IVY. Don't they sing?

REGGIE. Not enough . . . Come on, Charlie, let's go look at the car . . . I'm afraid it hasn't been out of the garage for ten years . . .

CHARLIE. You mean I really am in charge of a Silver Ghost Rolls-Royce?

REGGIE. Her name's Caprice . . . which, as I remember, is also her temperament.

He takes a sandwich.

Oh and Ivy . . .

IVY. Yes?

REGGIE. Just a tip for the future . . . I'm not sure if whelk sandwiches are quite the thing . . .

He exits. As CHARLIE *goes to exit, she passes* ROSALIND.

ROSALIND. Listen, I'm sorry I called you an oik . . . I actually think you're lucky being working class and having an accent and everything – I mean it makes you much more real and gritty than me as an actress. Gosh sorry, I mean, you are working class, aren't you?

CHARLIE. Yeah. But looking on the bright side, Ros – Your class control eighty-four per cent of the Nation's wealth . . .

ROSALIND. Gosh, do we?

Various people arrive in the rehearsal room. IVY *hands out sandwiches.* HETTY *arrives.*

HETTY. Back to work, girls . . . God in heaven, where is everyone?

JOSEPH *speaks. In his hand is a note.* IVY *is next to him.*

JOSEPH. Please don't be shooting the messenger. 'Unable to continue the show. Devastated.'

IVY. Ooh. It's from them three giggly girls from Central.

JOSEPH. 'P.S. We are off to play in *The Mikado* for ENSA. Real war work with real men! P.P.S. Miss Oak, we hate to mention it but you're a bad-tempered old . . . duck?'

IVY. 'Dyke' . . . oh . . . bogger.

HETTY *takes the letter, screws it up, and majestically tosses it aside.*

HETTY. In case anyone wants to know, I'm as neutral about sapphic women as I am prejudiced in favour of homosexual men. All I can say is that the combined acting talent of those three little girls was less conspicuous than the armpit hair of the common housefly.

Everyone applauds. FLORA *arrives out of breath.*

FLORA. Sorry I'm late – I was halfway out the door and the phone rang . . .

HETTY. Winston Churchill?

FLORA. Close. It was Jocelyn Thripp . . . D'you remember . . .
the recital? Anyway, she's got us our first booking! Actually,
it's not quite what we had in mind but she's absolutely
desperate – It's a W.I. event for orphans on the Isle of
Dogs – frightfully worthwhile – and the highlight was to
have been Am Dram *Christmas Carol* – but virtually the
whole cast's gone down with mumps. Anyway, it's
somewhere to do the show for the Ministry – I say, what's
wrong? . . .

HETTY (*handing* FLORA *the letter*). We still don't have a full
compliment. We've got Charlie, Rosalind, Gertrude, you
and me . . . that's all that's left . . . and we've only got ten
days . . . no, nine really.

FLORA. Oh what stinkers . . . And I'm afraid there is a tinsy
drawback I forgot to mention – Jocelyn Thripp always likes
to *appear* in her charity evenings . . . apparently she was
going to be the Ghost of Christmas Past and Mister
Fezziwig . . . and she likes to sing . . . as you may
remember . . . Mind you, we do rather need someone to
play the 'eld'.

HETTY. So be it . . . that makes six of us. Ivy – You've got a
splendid voice and no talent whatsoever in the kitchen . . .
What do you know about Theatre? Shakespeare plays?

IVY. Nothing, Miss Oaks. Oh, apparently they make very good
toilet paper . . .

HETTY. Spot on. Welcome to the company . . .

IVY. No, I couldn't . . . but what I really want to be is a spy or
a dancer like Josephine Baker – I don't want to be an
actress actually . . . Sorroy.

HETTY. Now listen to me, young lady . . . It's for the little
orphans and I know how much they will mean to you, Ivy,
and what a beacon you will be to them. But perhaps even
more importantly for you and certainly for us, this could be
your ticket out of the terrifying, nay, bewildering world of
crockery and cucumber sandwiches . . .

IVY. Well . . .

HETTY. Splendid. Now given the Ministry deadline, I believe
we are compelled to accept this engagement . . . but even with
the tonally erratic Miss Thripp, we still need one more . . .

There is a bristling pause.

ROSALIND. Well, I suppose there's always Mummy . . .

Theme tune to Children's Hour. *A microphone marked BBC.
A red light says* 'RECORDING'. *We are in a radio studio
presenting* Children's Hour. HELEN *is dragging on a
cigarette.*

HELEN (as Elsie, *little girl voice*). Oh dear, whatever shall
I do? If I run away, I shall never be able to find the treasure.
No, I must be brave . . . but it is a frightfully spooky forest
in this thunderstorm.

She makes thunder noises with a thunder sheet.

HETTY *and company enter and crowd as if peering
through a glass pane.*

Goodness, Mister Pirate, what are you doing here?

(As Bob, *the pirate.*) Why, stap my vitals. If it isn't the little
girl! I'm just cleanin' these here cutlasses . . .

She makes sound effects of cutlasses.

(Elsie.) Will you help me to find the treasure? . . . It belongs
to my grandfather and I know he'll give you a big reward . . .

(Bob.) Bless your heart . . . I'll just whet my whistle with
this 'ere bottle of rum . . . (*She makes a cork pop and she
swigs from a flask.*) I'll tell you what, little Elsie. Whoever
wrote this drivel should be made to walk the plank.

(Elsie.) You're quite right, Mister Pirate . . . he should be
secured by his terribly small privates and strung up from the
yard-arm . . .

The voice of KEITH *the producer comes across the
loudspeaker.*

KEITH. Sadly, that's all we've got time for today, children, but let's listen to this lovely ditty before we join our friends Goosie and Hennie . . .

He puts on child-friendly music.

Alright everybody, live transmission is stopped . . . God in heaven, what's going on, Helen? What on earth are you playing at? Has she been drinking again?

HELEN *speaks into the microphone in a mellow piano-bar style underscored by the music.*

HELEN. Girls and boys. Sometimes the person you love falls in love with someone else, and when that happens it's very sad indeed. It happened to me and I wrote this little song. It's called 'Bugger Off Keith, You Total Bastard'. I hope you'll both be very happy together.

KEITH (*across the loudspeaker*). I hope you'll be happy too, Helen. P.S. You're fired.

ROSALIND. I think Mummy's a teensy bit upset . . .

FLORA. But the super news is she's available . . .

HETTY. God in heaven . . .

ROSALIND. She might feel better after another drink . . .

The group reforms to create a crowded pub bar.

HELEN (*holding forth drunkenly*). Never Never. Never. First rule of acting, Rosalind, never work with children or dogs . . .

ROSALIND. The *Isle* of Dogs, Mummy, and it's *for* children.

HELEN. What do little children contribute to us – What? Nothing. Niente. What am I to them? . . . I'm one of those . . . haberdasher things . . . what do you call them . . . for pinning clothes?

FLORA. Dummy?

HELEN. Who are you? I'm ancient history . . . I'm cobwebs, Jesus . . . What's the big deal about the young? What about the over-forties, for Christ's sake . . . when did we become so meaningless?

ROSALIND. Mummy . . .

HELEN. I'm fascinated to hear, darling, why you want to be in a company where the only men you get to act with are women? It'll be like a nunnery on wheels . . . and anyway, what's the point of performing for dogs?

ROSALIND. No, Mummy, *on* the *Isle* of Dogs.

FLORA. Talking of animals, years ago I remember seeing you in a marvellous thing called *The Wibbly Wobbly Pig* – everyone thought it was the most delightful children's show they'd ever seen – Well, certainly Reggie and me . . .

HELEN. Who is this woman? *The Wibbly Wobbly Pig* was a pile of excrement . . . Believe me, if you want to entertain kids these days, you've got to be a big-eared mouse or a bloody munchkin . . .

HETTY. Helen . . . please . . . All I'm asking is a few days to give some deprived and lonely orphans a little happiness at this time of harrowing uncertainty . . .

Pause.

HELEN. Well, if it's for the little orphans, darling, then of course I'll do it.

Everyone freezes except HELEN *and* ROSALIND.

ROSALIND. No no, it wasn't like that.

HELEN. Wasn't it? Surely it was . . . I mean the gist . . . I can't be expected to remember exactly . . .

They replay the moment.

HETTY. Helen . . . please . . . All I'm asking is a few days to give some deprived and lonely orphans a little happiness at this time of harrowing uncertainty . . .

Pause.

HELEN. Sod off.

Everyone freezes except HELEN *and* ROSALIND.

Really? . . . Anyway, that should have been that. But as you know nothing's ever that simple in the shark-infested thorn-bush we know as . . . (*She drinks again.*) . . . 'The Business' . . . and Fate had other plans for me . . .

CHARLIE *unfreezes.*

CHARLIE. 'Ere we go . . .

HELEN. So there was I, innocently venturing my critical faculties on the latest offering from Hollywood . . . Quietly minding my own business . . .

CHARLIE. Sobering up after a liquid lunch.

HELEN. When I realised I had company.

Children's laughter. HETTY, FLORA, REGGIE, IVY, CHARLIE, ROSALIND, GERTRUDE *and* JOSEPH *are all sitting in a cinema watching* Snow White. HELEN *arrives at the back.*

The film has reached the crucial poisoned apple moment with the Wicked Queen arriving in disguise. The film breaks and, as everything goes black, the soundtrack switches off.

HETTY. Live by technology . . . you die by technology . . .

USHERETTE. Sorry – That's all for today, folks!

The sound of devastated children.

FLORA. How madly frustrating. Just look at all those dear little crests falling.

The scratchy 78 record of the National Anthem starts.

HETTY. God in heaven . . . no . . .

Suddenly HETTY *gets up onto the stage in front of the screen. The record stops.*

Well, this won't do, will it? Do we want the story to go on? Well, do we?

CHILDREN (*shouting*). YES!

HETTY. I don't think I heard the magic word?

CHILDREN. PLEASE.

HETTY. No. It's MAKE-BELIEVE. 'On your imaginary
forces work.' Usherette, shine your torch on me, would you?

*The light shines on her. The troupe watch in some terror as
she pulls her coat over her head and transforms herself into
a witch.*

I am the Wicked Queen.

The CHILDREN *boo.*

This – (*She holds up her purse.*) – is the poisoned apple . . .
Now where's Snow White? Is anyone home? Snow White?
Where are you, dear?

*Her cowardly troupe sink down in their chairs and look at
the floor.* HETTY *needs help or the idea will collapse.*

Snow White?

*There is an awful pause and then a little girl's voice we
have heard somewhere before.*

HELEN. Why, it's a dear sweet whiskery old beggar woman.
Come in and rest your legs.

HELEN *has spoken as Snow White. She pushes* ROSALIND
to go onto the stage.

Go on, darling, she needs a Snow White . . . you've got the
legs . . . you're supposed to be trained . . . think Shirley
Temple meets Celia Johnson . . .

CHILDREN. Hooray!

ROSALIND *stands there, speechless.*

HELEN (Snow White). I'm afraid all the dwarves off to work
have gone . . . so I'm just waiting for my prince to come . . .

ROSALIND (*takes over from* HELEN *as* Snow White). Oh
you dear, sweet, old beggar woman, do take tea with me . . .

HETTY (Wicked Queen). No, I can't come in . . . but I
brought you this lovely apple from my garden.

ROSALIND (Snow White). How very dear and sweet of you.

She goes to eat the apple.

CHILDREN. NO, IT'S POISONOUS! IT'S THE WICKED
QUEEN! DON'T EAT IT!

HETTY (Wicked Queen). Farewell, Snow White. (*Cackles.*)

ROSALIND swoons and falls.

But who's coming down the garden path? Could it be the
seven dwarves?

Her troupe all dive for cover in the audience. HELEN *is
thrilled.*

IVY. Oh bloody bogger it.

CHARLIE. Oh God, no . . .

HETTY (Wicked Queen). YES! It's a good percentage of the
seven dwarves. One, two, three, four, seven!

*FLORA, CHARLIE, IVY, REGGIE and JOSEPH are
volunteered.*

HELEN. Hooray! . . . Let's hear it for those dwarves! . . .
There's Wrinkly and Boozy and Deafy and Stinky . . .

*They come onstage singing and kneel behind ROSALIND
(Snow White). The CHILDREN cheer and sing along.*

FLORA (Bashful). Whatever happened to Snow White, she
won't wake up . . . Thingy . . . Grumpy . . . whoever you
are?

IVY (Grumpy). Don't ask me . . . Bashful . . . ask . . .
Sneezy . . .

REG (Sneezy). What? Oh . . . Aitishoo.

JOSEPH (Doc). Sneeze softly . . . wake her not . . .

FLORA (Bashful). Oh dear, there must be something we can
do. Perhaps if all the boys and girls clapped their hands and
said, 'I do believe in . . . in . . . ' What's that magic word?
Mi . . . Mi . . .

HELEN. Midgets!

FLORA (Bashful). 'Miracles' – it might just break the cruel spell. Will you children clap your hands if you believe in miracles?

CHILDREN (*clapping madly as with Tinkerbell*). I DO BELIEVE IN MIRACLES.

IVY (Grumpy). She's still not breathing . . . she's not breathing . . . what can we do?

JOSEPH (Doc). Now boast thee death in thy possession lies a lass unparalleled.

FLORA (Bashful). Come on, darling . . . wake up angel.

IVY (Grumpy). Oh please don't let her die . . . please let a miracle happen.

JOSEPH (Doc). . . . Speak thou for my heart is full . . .

DOPEY. Perhaps if I . . . perhaps a kiss . . .

> CHARLIE *leans down and tenderly kisses* ROSALIND. GERTRUDE *plays 'waking-up' music on the piano.*

FLORA (Bashful). Oh how wonderful . . . a miracle . . . Snow White is coming back to life . . .

CHILDREN. HOORAY!

> *Everyone freezes except* HETTY *and* FLORA.

HETTY. It was certainly the bonding experience we'd been looking for, wasn't it, Bashful? By the end of the show we had at least a hundred little volunteer dwarves happily singing 'Someday My Prince Will Come' and a delighted captive audience . . .

FLORA. And then the real miracle happened . . .

> HELEN *steps forward.*

HELEN. Only eight days – and I want my own dressing room.

> *A surge of hectic activity as the sound of bombs falling.*

HETTY (*reads*). 'My darling, who knows if we will be allowed to continue now that the Germans are intent on

bombing London, but 'we carry on, we carry on'. I think
the Artemis Players might well give the Crummles
Company a run for their money. We are about to be the full
compliment so I'd like to say to whoever is up there
deciding our fates . . . "for this relief much thanks" . . . and
please keep watching over my own beloved soldier.'

*Everyone in a rehearsal room busy making props, costumes,
up ladders, etc.*

HETTY. Right, these are general notes on yesterday's stagger
so that when and if Miss Thripp ever gets here, we can lead
by example . . . Flora. Stop thinking and feel . . . It's about
as moving as a broken fingernail . . .

FLORA. I'm sorry . . . It's just there was a full moon and I
couldn't sleep . . .

HETTY. May I state here and now that I am having no truck
with time-of-the-month excuses . . . on any front . . .
otherwise this whole enterprise will be held hostage by our
collective hormones . . . Ivy – stop looking down while you
act . . . you seem to be playing every scene opposite Mickey
Rooney . . .

IVY. Sorroy. Can I just ask . . . what does it mean 'Macduff
was from his mother's womb untimely ripped'? I've never
got that bit . . .

JOSEPH. It means, Ivy, that the mother is dying before the
baby is being born. So what can they do to save the baby?

IVY. What? You mean they cut the baby out of her? Bloody
bogger . . .

HETTY. Now if I might . . .

JOCELYN THRIPP *arrives unnoticed.*

IVY. Sorroy . . .

HETTY. Charlie – stop all that palaver with your eyebrows . . .
Helen – very good but concentrate on your own
performance . . . and now all of you – stop pausing between
words. We're not Americans . . .

JOCELYN. Goodness, there's no flum about you, Miss Oak . . . straight from the hip . . .

HETTY. Ah! I'd like to introduce the final member of the Artemis Players – Miss Jocelyn Thripp, who suffered a small setback in joining us but we're thrilled to have her with us at last.

People applaud.

JOCELYN. Dear me – It's frightfully naughty of you to rope me in to your troupe but anyway, I'm game, and I think it's a super idea doing Shakespeare – for me, he's right up there with P.G. Wodehouse . . . I'm just sorry my dratted leg's kept me 'hors de combat' till today. Now if I find myself in the vicinity of a kettle, shall I pop it on?

HETTY. Not yet, Miss Thripp. We have a great deal of work to do and, may I remind us all, only six remaining days to do it . . . Carry on everyone . . . Joseph –

HELEN (*drinking from a hip flask*). Oh what about notes for Rosalind? I'd say it's a remarkable achievement that after three inordinately expensive years at the RADA, she's emerged with no passion whatsoever . . . Her words fall like . . . dead birds from the sky . . . thunk . . . thunk . . . thunk . . .

HETTY. May I continue?

HELEN. Just trying to be helpful.

HETTY. Joseph, explain the scenic layout to Miss Thripp . . . the rest of you, carry on . . .

JOSEPH. Costumes in corridor behind stage . . . Remember kitchen-side is being left-stage, bathroom-side is right-stage though when standing onstage, left-stage is right-stage and versa-vice . . . and proppings table will be near prompting-corner and not forgetting up-stage is backstage and down-stage is front-stage . . .

HETTY. Well, I think that's clear . . . Now to help you identify all of us, I will take you through the allocation of roles in the Scottish tragedy . . . For convenience, I use the name

Walter Plinge for 'small parts as allocated' . . . and any crowd appearances will be referred to as 'the salad'. I have had the effrontery to cast myself as the Thane . . .

CHARLIE (*whispers*). It's her funeral . . .

She wanders amongst them.

HETTY. Mrs Helen Irving here is playing my wife, Lady Macbeth, Hecate and . . .

HELEN. And a severed head . . .

HETTY. Miss Flora Pelmet – Banquo, Ross, Walter Plinge . . .

HELEN. Actually, sorry, but why can't I just play Lady M.? I find it impossible to leap in and out of character like some frenzied tiddlywink . . .

HETTY. Later, Helen . . . Rosalind – Lennox, Macduff, Walter Plinge. Ivy – First Witch, Second Murderer, salad. Charlie – Second Witch, Lady Macduff, Seyton and Plinge except the Cream-Faced Loon . . . who will have to be played by our resident musician, Mrs Gertrude Rosenbaum, because we're all tied-up at that point. And finally, you of course, Miss Thripp – Third Witch, First Murderer, Old King Duncan, the Old Man, Old Siward . . .

JOCELYN. D'you know, I see the Third Witch as rather young and racy . . .

HETTY. Now obviously today we must begin by reading your scenes in the play, Miss Thripp . . . but on its feet, as it were, . . . Let's start with the Murderers' scene . . . page 46 . . .

JOCELYN. Splendid . . . and what page is tea-time?

They all shuffle into position with JOSEPH *on the book, etc.*

HETTY. Alright, Murderers quietly in from up-centre.

CHARLIE (Lady Macduff). What are these faces?

JOCELYN. Is it me? Oh dear, where are my glasses? Ooh, on my head . . . I'm such a silly . . . Right . . . (First Murderer.) Wh . . . wh . . . where's your husband?

HETTY. I'm not sure the Murderer needs a stammer.

JOCELYN. It was working awfully well for Mister Fezziwig.

HETTY. D'you know, I'm a great believer in less is more . . . Carry on.

JOCELYN. Okey doke . . . (First Murderer.) Where's your husband?

CHARLIE (Lady Macduff). I hope in no place so unsanctified where such as thou mayst find him.

JOCELYN (First Murderer). He's a traitor . . .

ROSALIND (Son). Thou liest, thou shag-haired villain.

JOCELYN. Is that right? Sounds frightfully rude.

IVY (Second Murderer). What? You egg. Young fry of treachery.

Silence.

JOSEPH. It's you, Mrs Thripp . . .

JOCELYN. Oh . . . where? . . .

ROSALIND. Before I say 'He has killed me, mother'.

JOCELYN. How can you speak if he's killed you? Ours not to reason why . . . Run away!

ROSALIND. No. I say 'run away'. (Son.) Run away!

JOCELYN. Ah! Now I do hope you're not expecting Jesse Owens in pursuit . . . because, you see, I've got this rather gammy leg . . .

HETTY. Stop . . .

JOCELYN. Is that tea?

HETTY. No. Yes. I'm past caring. Maybe the witches will be less controversial. Joseph, could you set up to go from the top.

Everyone leaves except HELEN *and* ROSALIND. *As* HELEN *goes to leave,* JOSEPH *pops his head round the corner.*

JOSEPH. Ros, could you clear swords please . . .

ROSALIND *picks up two swords.*

HELEN. Yes, for God's sake do something useful.

ROSALIND *corners* HELEN *with the swords.*

ROSALIND. Don't you ever talk to me like that . . . d'you hear me? Never never never . . .

ROSALIND *plays cat and mouse with* HELEN.

HELEN. What are you doing? Don't hurt me. Please don't hurt me.

ROSALIND. Kneel down at my feet . . . DO IT . . .

HELEN *does as she's told.*

Now apologise for all the years you've treated me like I'm nobody and nothing . . . say 'I'm so sorry, Ros, my darling precious girl'.

HELEN. I'm so sorry, Ros, my precious darling girl.

She stands up and goes to leave. The scene replays.
JOSEPH *pops his head round the corner.*

JOSEPH. Ros, could you clear swords please . . .

HELEN. Yes, for God's sake do something useful.

As HELEN *exits,* CHARLIE *enters.* ROSALIND *sits down amongst the swords and weeps.*

CHARLIE. What's the matter with you, you miserable cow?

ROSALIND. Why is she so horrid to me? She's such a liar and she's so bloody selfish . . .

CHARLIE. Yeah well, if you're Joan Crawford those count as talents.

HELEN *suddenly appears at the door.*

HELEN. I hate to interrupt your little tête-à-tête . . . but our dear leader was wondering if the soubrettes would mind going to buy some milk . . . oh, and half a bottle of gin . . . strictly for theatrical purposes you understand.

HETTY *comes through the door. As they exit,* HELEN *does a little heel-click as she goes.*

HELEN. Herr Kommandant.

HETTY starts to pick up the swords and suddenly breaks down in tears. FLORA comes back in with a tray.

FLORA. Now Ivy's gone and broken the jug so there's no more milk . . . Hetty, are you alright?

HETTY. No, Flora, I'm not . . . We should stop this now.

FLORA. Stop . . . What are you saying?

HETTY. This isn't it . . . it's not what we meant at all . . . Our dream of something inspirational . . . it's turned into a nightmare . . . we couldn't inspire Emily Pankhurst's dog . . . Let's stop now . . .

FLORA. Hetty, listen to me. We've come so far and we're in so deep that, in the words of Macbeth, 'Returning were as tedious as go o'er'.

HETTY laughs.

All we need is a little luck.

Gracie Fields sings 'Wish Me Luck as You Wave Me Goodbye'.

Total chaos of loading up/building the Rolls-Royce with hampers of costumes, props, cases, etc. – all of them piling in and singing along.

They are setting up for the performance in the pub hall.

HELEN. Luck? When Mister Fezziwig said we were performing in the Globe, I assumed it was a theatre.

CHARLIE. But it wasn't.

HELEN. It was a public house . . . the place was rancid and it reeked of alcohol . . .

HELEN swigs from her hip flask as the rest continue to set up.

CHARLIE. And anyway, we were performing in the pub hall at the back – stuffed with piles of clothes and furniture salvaged from the bombing-raids on the docks. But then our luck changed . . .

HELEN. It got worse. Gertrude and Joseph finally got a date for their tribunal . . .

JOCELYN. It was the day of the performance!

ROSALIND (*staring at a bowl*). And then Ivy used beetroot juice and treacle for the blood.

JOCELYN. Which definitely wasn't right . . .

IVY. Well, Joseph normally did the proppings . . .

ROSALIND. Not to mention the fact he had all the beards and moustaches.

FLORA. But then, as luck would have it, I found a perfectly manky old coat in the boot of the car . . . which I cut into little squares and . . .

CHARLIE. Alakazan! Facial-hair crisis was solved . . .

HETTY *arrives clutching a very alopecian fur coat. She is livid.*

HETTY. Good God, Flora. Just because you have a cousin who is profligate with Rolls-Royces doesn't mean you can treat everyone and everything as your property . . .

FLORA. I'm terribly sorry . . . mea tonsorially culpa . . . but – (*Genuinely distressed.*) – you do only ever wear the one coat . . .

HETTY. Oh stop snivelling. This is no place for uncontrolled emotions. Why can't you let them go on the stage? . . .

FLORA. I'm sorry but I don't actually think I can schedule my humanity . . .

HETTY. Honestly, Flora, this is no time to pick a fight . . .

REGGIE *appears in a lather.*

REGGIE. Flora – Hetty – could you . . . ?

They whisper urgently.

ROSALIND. Whatever it is . . . good luck, Mummy.

HELEN. Jesus, don't wish me good luck, you idiot.

ROSALIND. Why not?

HELEN. It's incredibly bad luck.

CHARLIE. It's probably something to do with the man from the Ministry . . . I heard him picking up his ticket . . . He looked a right snotty twerp . . . probably one of your relatives . . .

FLORA. Listen gang . . . attention please. It's ten minutes to the half when they will be opening the house, so we have to think clearly and act quickly. Apparently the Rosenbaums are still at their tribunal so I'm afraid they won't be here for the show or possibly one stage worse, they'll be on their way to the Isle of Man.

HETTY. This means we are without music and our Stage Manager. No no, listen . . . calm down. Miss Pelmet and I propose the following contingency plans. We will put up a list of essential sound effects and allocate those cues according to whoever is free. Check for a list in the prompt corner. I will take full responsibility for all lighting operation and the interval colour changes.

She holds up her big leather lighting gloves.

FLORA. I will deal with the smoke-machine and assist swift costume changes. Reggie has agreed to be occasional music and prompter. (*Applause.*) On a lesser note, we're also without a Cream-Faced Loon . . .

REGGIE. Oh surely your friend Mrs Chumley could step in . . . she's been caught up in the theatre world for years.

FLORA. No, she hasn't . . .

REGGIE. Yes, I heard she played bridge with Sybil Thorndike's cousin . . .

FLORA. Anyway, she does decoupage on Thursdays . . . Why don't you do it?

REGGIE. Absolutely not . . . I gave my all with Sneezy . . . Anyway, I was hoping to catch bits and pieces with my cine-camera . . . for posterity . . .

HELEN. As if posterity didn't have enough on its plate.

HETTY. Right – we've got a few minutes left. Time for a brief company warm-up. Let's begin with the floor exercise.

HELEN. Treat jostles with treat . . .

They lie on the filthy floor, making low vibrating notes.

HETTY. Breathe and hum – and breathe and aah . . . open open . . . find those low notes . . .

REGGIE. Hetty . . . could I have a quick word?

HETTY. Flora . . . take over . . .

He takes HETTY *aside.*

REGGIE. You don't have any family in active service, do you, dear? . . . I know you're not married but . . .

HETTY. No . . .

REGGIE. No, I didn't think so . . . it's just that this telegram arrived at home today and . . . well, one gets so . . . I mean you've got more than enough to cope with . . . Anyway . . . I'd better go and befriend the gramophone . . .

He leaves. HETTY *stares at the unopened telegram, puts it in her bra next to her heart, then strides amongst the group.*

HETTY. Alright, breathe and relax. Now, I know the man from the Ministry is in the audience but take risks . . . otherwise it's pointless . . . be brave enough to make fools of your-selves . . . And one last thing. I know this is an uncomfortable topic right now but . . . You're all totally useless at dying. Try to imagine how it feels – as the light goes out. Painful? Perhaps. Terrifying? Probably. And then the light slowly fades, or you burst into the sky and the stars . . . Not – (*She demonstrates.*) Arhhhhhh! Thud.

Everyone laughs.

JOCELYN. I had a little nephew who drowned. Such a tiny body – ah well. My sister Mary said, 'Think of it like this – you live, you love, and when God catches your eye, it's time to go.'

There's silence. Then they hear the deafening sound of a plane going overhead. They start to exit.

HETTY. One last thing . . . We've all been under pressure, and tempers have been frayed, but I just want you to know there isn't anyone I'd rather have at my side today . . . I want you to know that.

Pub piano. The MAYOR *totters on in a Santa hat to applause.*

MAYOR (*full of Christmas cheer*). The Lady Mayoress and I are very honoured to be here . . . it's lovely to see this pub hall being put to such good service. Last time there was a 'do' in the Globe it turned into a right rough-house, didn't it, Eileen? But the good news is we're going to have the Arsenic Players and Mister William Shakespeare's *Macbeth*. Ooh, am I allowed to say that? Anyway, I'm sure the show will be absolutely on a par with last year's *Puss in Boots* . . . and we're going to have a sing-a-long and some grub at half-time . . . so at least that's something to look forward to! I see we're about to kick off . . . So I give you . . . the one and only, Ladies and Gentlemen . . . The Artichoke Players . . .

The lights dim. Spooky shadows appear.

In the wings FLORA *is doing thunder and operates a small overacting smoke-machine.* HETTY *is manning the lighting switchboard. To begin with, the image of the witches looks superbly convincing.*

IVY (First Witch). When shall we three meet again? In thunder, lighting or in rain?

CHARLIE (Second Witch). When the hurlyburly's done . . . When the battle's lost and won.

JOCELYN (Third Witch). That will be ere the set of sun.

IVY (First Witch, *coughing*). Where the place? Upon the heath.

They are virtually obliterated by smoke.

CHARLIE (Second Witch). There to meet with Macbeth . . .

ALL. Fair is foul and foul is fair. Hover through the fog and filthy air . . .

JOCELYN (*audibly*). The smoke's got in my eyes . . . I can't . . .

The audience starts to cough.

HETTY (Macbeth). So foul and fair a day I have not seen.

FLORA (Banquo). What are these, so wither'd and so wild in their attire . . .

HETTY (Macbeth). Speak, if you can.

JOCELYN (Third Witch, *coughing*). I can't . . .

HETTY (Macbeth). What are you?

IVY (First Witch). All hail Macbeth! Hail to thee, Thane of Glamis!

CHARLIE (Second Witch). All hail Macbeth! Hail to thee, Thane of Cawdor!

JOCELYN (Third Witch). Stay . . . mine eyes do call me hence . . . (*Whispers.*) . . . won't be a jiffy . . . sorry . . .

REGGIE (*on prompt script*). Wrong . . .

JOCELYN backs out rapidly.

HETTY (Macbeth). Wither is she vanished?

FLORA (Banquo). Into the air . . . as breath into the wind.

HETTY (Macbeth). Would she had stay'd . . .

FLORA (Banquo). I' the name of truth,
Are ye fantastical, or that indeed
Which outwardly ye show? . . .
If you can look into . . .

JOCELYN hastily comes back on doing a strange dance. She has put on her glasses.

JOCELYN (Third Witch). All hail, Macbeth, that shalt be king hereafter . . . sorry.

IVY (First Witch). Lesser than Macbeth and greater.

CHARLIE (Second Witch). Not so happy, yet much happier.

JOCELYN (Third Witch, *coughing fit*). . . . kings though
(*Coughing.*) . . . none . . . (*Coughing.*)

REGGIE. Wrong . . .

They exit.

FLORA (Banquo). Stay you imperfect speakers . . .

In the wings, CHARLIE, *dressed as the Porter,* ROSALIND
as Macduff, go through their fight with their forefingers.

ROSALIND. Left right, left right, spin and lunge.

CHARLIE. Sweep, and spin, shoulder left, cut to the knee.

ROSALIND. The waist.

CHARLIE. The knee.

ROSALIND. It's going a bit better, isn't it?

CHARLIE. Evens . . .

Onstage. Knocking.

HETTY (Macbeth). Whence is that knocking?
How is't with me when every noise appals me?
Will all great Neptune's ocean wash this blood
Clean from my hand? No; this my hand will rather
The multitudinous seas incarnadine,
Making the green one red.

HELEN *enters as Lady Macbeth.*

HELEN (Lady Macbeth).
My hands are of your colour; but I shame
To wear a heart so white . . . I hear a knocking
At the south entry. Retire we to our chamber.
A little water clears us of this deed.
How easy is it then?

HETTY (Macbeth).
To know my deed, 'twere best not know myself.
Wake Duncan with thy knocking! I would thou couldst!

CHARLIE *enters as the Porter.*

In the wings, they discover they cannot wipe off the blood.

HELEN. The blood won't wipe off . . . Jesus what will we do? Everyone will know we murdered him so there's no plot left . . .

HETTY. Try pulling down your sleeves.

They try to no avail. FLORA *is madly knocking away.*

FLORA. Nil desperandum, I have an idea. Ivy, keep knocking.

CHARLIE *is onstage as the Porter with* ROSALIND *as Macduff.*

HETTY *reappears as Macbeth, wearing the big leather lighting gloves. They look aghast.*

HETTY (Macbeth). Good morrow both.

ROSALIND (Macduff). Is the king stirring within there?

HETTY (Macbeth). Not yet. *Silence.* I'll bring you to him.

The drone of planes in the sky above cross-fades into applause.

Applause. The MAYOR *returns. Now well and truly drunk.*

MAYOR. Well, I think there's something in there for everyone . . . Now I'm very happy to announce that the mince-pies are ready . . . and for those of you a little bit worried about the kiddies' bed-times . . . the good news is . . . the second half's much shorter!

JOSEPH *and* GERTRUDE *have returned. Everyone is putting on their beards and moustaches.* REGGIE *arrives with his camera.*

FLORA. Welcome back our fellow citizens, the Rosenbaums, who are now officially 'Category C, exempt from all restrictions applicable to enemy aliens'.

General cheering.

JOSEPH. It is truly a good deed in a naughty world. But how is it with you?

HETTY. It's been farcical . . .

ALL. No . . . no.

HETTY. . . . an unmitigated disaster.

> HETTY *takes out the telegram. She puts it back unopened.*

IVY. It's all been a bit barmy.

HETTY. However, we have our dear friends back with us, and we have facial hair. So there is no excuse this half. We have everything to play for. And remember, speak from the heart, feel from the heart . . .

Scenes underscored by GERTRUDE *with* JOSEPH *in the wings.*

Everyone is acting really well.

HELEN (Lady Macbeth).
How now, my lord! Why do you keep alone,
Of sorriest fancies your companions making,
Using those thoughts which should indeed have died
With them they think on? What's done is done . . .

HETTY (Macbeth).
We have scotched the snake, not killed it . . .
Better be with the dead,
Whom we, to gain our peace, have sent to peace,
Than on the torture of the mind to lie
In restless ecstasy. Duncan is in his grave;
After life's fitful fever he sleeps well.

HELEN (Lady Macbeth). Come on . . .
Gentle my lord, sleek o'er your rugged looks.

HETTY (Macbeth).
Treason has done his worst; nor steel, nor poison,
Malice domestic, foreign levy, nothing
Can touch him further.

HELEN (Lady Macbeth). You must leave this . . .

HETTY (Macbeth).
O full of scorpions is my mind, dear wife!
Thou knowest that Banquo and his Fleance lives . . .

HELEN (Lady Macbeth).
But in them nature's copy's not eterne . . .

HETTY (Macbeth). There's comfort yet.
Ere to black Hecate's summons
The shard-borne beetle with his drowsy hums
Hath rung night's drowsy peal, there shall be done
A deed of dreadful note.

HELEN (Lady Macbeth, *whispers*). What's to be done?

HETTY (Macbeth).
Be innocent of the knowledge, dearest chuck,
Till thou applaud the deed . . .

Seyton and Macduff (CHARLIE *and* ROSALIND) *cross the
stage doing a superbly dextrous sword fight. As they reach
the wings they hug and congratulate each other.*

FLORA (Ross). Your son, my lord, has paid a soldier's debt.
He only lived but till he was a man . . .
But like a man he died.

JOCELYN (Siward). Had I as many sons as I have hairs,
I would not wish them to a fairer death . . .

Macbeth and Macduff (HETTY *and* ROSALIND) *are
fighting.*

HETTY (Macbeth). I bear a charmed life which must not yield
To one of woman born.

ROSALIND (Macduff). Despair thy charm;
And let the angel whom thou still has served
Tell thee, Macduff was from his mother's womb
Untimely ripped . . .

HETTY (Macbeth). Accursed be the tongue that tells me so . . .
Lay on, Macduff,
And damn'd be him that first cries, 'Hold, enough!'

Exit fighting. Alarms, trumpets, etc. and cheering applause.

The cast come offstage after their curtain call. REGGIE *is
filming them with his cine-camera.*

REGGIE. Smile! Shall I give you something to smile about? The Ministry man has just told me he was so impressed with the show and the enthusiastic response that he'll be sending a letter to confirm that the Artemis Players will be getting approval, endorsement and *money*!

Cheers, etc. In the background, the National Anthem plays out in the hall.

HETTY. God in heaven, let's get out of here . . .

FLORA. Hang on! We've got a surprise for you . . .

ROSALIND. Quick quick, come on everyone.

IVY. Don't go away, Miss Oak.

Everyone exits excitedly into the wings.

HETTY. Can I just say one brief word?

CHARLIE. That'll be a first!

JOCELYN. In a minute!

They disappear. HETTY is left alone. She puts her hand in her pocket, pulls out the telegram.

HETTY (*whispers*). Not today . . . Oh please Lord . . . not today.

FLORA reappears.

FLORA. Oh Hetty. We did it . . . I'm coming . . . Oh Lor', is that your telegram? Haven't you opened it yet?

HETTY opens it and reads.

HETTY. 'Screw your courage to the sticking post and we'll not fail . . . '

FLORA. It's from me . . . and all the gang.

HETTY. ' . . . your fellow lesbians'.

FLORA. What? No no, I said 'thespians'. Oh mea annunciatorily culpa . . .

HETTY hugs FLORA.

HETTY. Oh bless you . . . you see, Flora, I have a secret . . . and it's time I . . .

CHARLIE. Flora!!

FLORA. Sorry, the girls need me for the surprise . . . don't go away.

HETTY shuts her eyes.

HETTY. Oh thank God . . . oh thank God. Nothing else matters as long as you are safe.

They return with a Union Jack and song sheets – one of which they hand to HETTY, all filmed by REGGIE.

FLORA. Miss Thripp has kindly agreed to suspend her eagerly awaited rendition of 'Only God Can Make a Tree' to lead us in a new anthem penned by our dear friends and fellow citizens, the Rosenbaums, to celebrate the birth of the Artemis Players.

They launch into song.

ALL (*singing*). This throne of kings, this scept'red isle.
   This earth of majesty,
   This seat of Mars, this precious stone
   Set in the silver sea.
   This Eden, demi-paradise,
   Renowned by word and deed,
   This blessed plot, this earth, this realm,
   This world, this happy breed.

As music continues.

HETTY. Thank you all for everything. This is just the beginning of the adventure. We may permit ourselves a brief period of rejoicing but then our mission during the next year is to take our heritage throughout the length and breadth of Britain and into the hearts of each and every person we meet along the way. Not just Shakespeare but Shaw, the Mysteries, Dickens, Noël Coward, A.A. Milne . . . How we will achieve this I don't know, but I know we *will* because we have proved to ourselves we can . . .

Applause.

No no, none of that. As I wrote in a letter just two days ago to Mister Winston Churchill asking for his patronage for our endeavour – we have nothing to offer but blood, toil, sweat and tears . . .

ALL (*singing*). This Eden, demi-paradise,
Renowned by word and deed,
This blessed plot, this earth, this realm,
This world, this happy breed . . .
This blessed plot, this earth, this realm,
This world, this happy breed.

As the anthem reaches a choral climax with the company in ecstatic full voice, there is blackout and silence.

End of Act One.

ACT TWO

A spectral procession emerges from amongst the costume rails,
more or less returned to their starting places. They do a slow
Busby Berkeley dance to Noël Coward's 'If Love Were All'
heard distantly and through a reverberation that makes the
music plaintive. As the dancers depart, there is rousing music
as the Pathe news flickers into life from the projector (or
simply as sound).

NEWSREEL VOICE. . . . so with our American chums
alongside and our front foot forward, September 1944 may
see the final drive against Jerry. Go get 'em lads! Give 'em
some Yankeedoodledandy! Back home, the British people
are as ready as ever to play their part in the war effort . . .
or should I say parts! 'All the world's a stage' and here at
home a truer word was ne'ry spake. The Artemis Players are
dressed and ready for action. They've travelled thousands
of miles bringing Shakespeare and friends across Britain in
their trusty Rolls-Royce – honk honk – look out! These
seven plucky girls really are stepping into men's shoes,
bringing culture to the people for the price of a bag of
humbugs! Keep up the good work, girls, and careful! Don't
fall off that stage!!

The company emerge from all over the store using it to
maximum theatrical effect – changing costumes – using
spotlights and props – arriving through trap-doors —
through costume rails like mini curtained prosceniums –
using the ladders and walkways – creating an eruption of
mayhem. (/ indicates points of overlap.)

ROSALIND. O Romeo Romeo, wherefore art thou / Romeo?

HELEN. O Julius Caesar, thou art mighty / yet.

JOCELYN. Cordelia / Cordelia.

IVY. O Tamar, thou bearst a woman's face.

FLORA. You are called plain Kate.

HETTY. I'll call thee Hamlet.

CHARLIE. And I thy Rosalind.

HELEN. Is your name Shylock?

JOCELYN. I Snug the Joiner am.

FLORA. Let me be Thisbe.

CHARLIE. And I thy Rosalind.

JOCELYN. I'll call thee Hamlet.

HELEN. You are called plain Kate.

HETTY. I am Antony yet.

CHARLIE. Robin Goodfellow, are you not he?

ROSALIND. And let the babbling gossip of the air cry out
Olivia.

IVY. For never was a story of more woe
Than this of Romeo and her . . . oops sorroy.

Company:

FLORA. It's incredible how many places we'd been to by
1944 . . .

JOCELYN. . . . a repertoire of thirty-five plays . . .

IVY. . . . sixteen of them Shakespeares . . .

HETTY. . . . performed up to four times a day . . .

ROSALIND. . . . a different play each time . . .

JOCELYN. . . . ten o'clock, *Saint Joan* . . .

FLORA. . . . one o'clock, *Blithe Spirit* . . .

ROSALIND. . . . teatime, *Oedipus Rex* . . .

HETTY. . . . seven-thirty, *Richard II* . . .

IVY. . . . not to mention the odd late-night revue.

HELEN *and* CHARLIE (*as George and Lily*) *launch into a vaudeville song.*

HELEN (George). La la la la-la la la la.

CHARLIE (Lily). Here, what are you singing about?

HELEN (George). What's the matter with my singing?

CHARLIE (Lily). What isn't the matter with it?

HELEN (George). Don't you think I could do anything useful with my voice?

CHARLIE (Lily). Well, it might be useful in case of fire!

HELEN (George). Keep it clean. Keep it fresh. Keep it fragrant.

REGGIE.
From Land's End . . .
to Lochgilphead.

JOSEPH.
Weston-super-Mare . . .
to Balleymalloy.

St Joan:

HETTY (Archbishop). Joan – You stand alone, absolutely alone. Trusting in your own impiety in hiding all these sins under the cloak of a trust in God.

IVY (Joan). Do not think you can frighten me by telling me that I am alone. France is alone; and God is alone. I will dare and dare and dare until I die. And so, God be with me.

Members of the troupe perform a short scene from a classic children's story (e.g., Peter Pan *or* Winnie the Pooh).

REGGIE. Pontefract . . .
Abergavenny.

JOSEPH. Chipping Camden . . .
Clacton-on-Sea.

A Midsummer Night's Dream:

FLORA (Quince). This green plot shall be our stage . . .

A siren.

(*Out of character.*) Oh hell's bells . . .

She exits.

JOCELYN. Skegness.

IVY. Ullapool.

JOCELYN. Saffron Walden.

IVY. Barrow-in-Furness.

JOCELYN. How did we do it?

IVY. What kept us going?

Oliver Twist:

HELEN (Fagin). Well, Dodger, I hope you've been working hard, my dears.

CHARLIE (Artful Dodger). Oh yes, Fagin, hard as nails.

HELEN (Fagin). Very good boys, aren't they, Oliver?

ROSALIND (Oliver). Oh yes sir, thank you sir, very good indeed sir.

ALL. Yes Hetty,
    No Hetty,
    Three bags full Hetty.
    Oh yes Hetty,
    Thank you Hetty,
    Very good indeed Hetty.

A montage of overlapping Shakespearean lines:

HETTY (Hamlet). To be or not to be / that is the question.

IVY (Ophelia). What means this, my lord?

JOCELYN (Touchstone). With a hey and a ho / and a hey nonny no –

FLORA (Gertrude). Alas! He's mad –

HELEN (Rosalind). Do you not know I am a woman? When I think I must speak –

CHARLIE (Soothsayer). Beware Beware / Beware –

ROSALIND (Lady Percy). For God's sake, go not to these wars –

JOCELYN (Chorus, *Henry V*). Now all the youth of England are on fire –

HELEN (Macbeth). It will have blood – Blood will have / blood –

CHARLIE (Thersites). Lechery lechery – nothing but wars and lechery –

IVY (Claudio). Ay but to die and go we know not where –

JOCELYN (Ghost, *Hamlet*). Oh horrible horrible / . . . most horrible –

FLORA (Lear). Howl Howl / Howl –

HETTY (Henry V). On, on, you noble English –

ALL (Henry V). For England, Harry and Saint George! –

HETTY (*reads*). 'My dearest darling. Yesterday we did our thousandth performance with a matinée of *Julius Caesar* . . . Oh Crispian, I want to tell you it was wonderful, but I'm afraid it was one of the unhappiest days of my life . . . '

The costume rails move again to create three sides of a square.

School bell. Sound of primary school and a drip. FLORA, ROSALIND, CHARLIE, HELEN *and* JOCELYN *arrive in a primary school cloakroom with plimsoll bags on pegs, etc.* CHARLIE *is packing things into a hamper. All still carrying or wearing bits of* Julius Caesar *costume.* (*By now they have all spent so much time together, they often overlap or finish each other's sentences.*)

JOCELYN. Well, we've been in worse places – but oh, I wish we didn't have to sleep next to the lavatories . . .

CHARLIE. Think of it as 'en-suite' . . . And looking on the bright side, it's not every day we get the luxury of a plimsoll bag for a pillow . . .

FLORA. I fear this place is a stranger to Vim . . .

HELEN. What a dump . . . this is so completely it . . . I've had enough . . .

She claims her sleeping space – a large drip lands on her head.

Oh Jesus, there's a bloody drip . . . look . . . someone get a bucket, Rosalind . . . Right, Hetty's stupid dog can sleep there . . . serve it right for being a dog . . .

ROSALIND *goes and gets a bucket and places it under the unrelenting drip.*

(*Impatiently.*) What?

ROSALIND. It's nothing – It's just that Ivy's cooking tonight . . .

General groans as they start to change.

HELEN. God, I'm so depressed I've even lost the will to smoke . . .

A man (BERT) *sticks his head round the corner.*

BERT. Hi gang! 'It's that man again! It's that man again . . .'

JOCELYN. 'Shall I do you now, sir?'

BERT. No, it's not Tommy Handley, it's . . . oops! Don't mind me, ladies – I'm a married man myself . . . I'm just locking up now . . . but my wife gave me these for you and she wanted you to know she loved the show and so did my daughter . . . thought it was definitely worth more than the fivepence . . . so she gave me these to give you . . . and these thank-you letters from a few of the kids . . .

He hands them the letters, a box of eggs, a pot of jam and some biscuits.

ALL. Eggs! Oh God, eggs! (*etc.*)

FLORA. Do thank your wife . . . that's very generous, isn't it, girls?

CHARLIE *and* ROSALIND. Oh yes sir, thank you sir, very good indeed sir.

BERT. And if you're up for it, there's a bit of a dance in the town hall tonight where yours truly will be doing some songs at the microphone, y'know, loved ones, neglected ones . . . TTFN . . .

He leaves passing IVY *who comes in carrying a vast bunch of flowers. She is still dressed in her costume but has little wings.*

IVY. You what?

BERT. Ta Ta For Now . . . Look out or you'll get pollen on your wings!

JOCELYN. My, look at you – busting out in flowers . . .

FLORA. You'd better get changed.

IVY. Do you like the wings?

CHARLIE. Give us a twirl.

IVY. One of the teachers gave them me and I just picked these . . . Ooh my head feels all balloony. I'm in such a funny mood, I don't know whether to laugh or cry . . .

HELEN. Nor do I – you're cooking tonight . . .

IVY. Oh bogger – sorroy . . . Is it alright if it's spam sandwiches?

JOCELYN. We could toast them on the Primus stove with our swords . . . we can have them with the eggs . . .

CHARLIE gets out a Primus stove and puts it in the middle like a camp fire. IVY returns the bucket with flowers to the same place and puts on the eggs in a kettle. ROSALIND collects the costumes and puts them neatly in a hamper . . . FLORA reads out a child's letter.

FLORA. Do listen to this . . . 'Thank you very much for having us to your play . . . It was more fun than Arithmetic but not as good as football. I liked Mark Antony best because she was the prettiest.' How dotey! Oh and he's made us a . . . a something . . . out of raffia paper!

HELEN snatches the letter and reads it.

JOCELYN (*darning a sock*). Bless them . . . If you're ever looking for God, He's there in children's eyes.

HELEN. What does this little moron know about anything? He can't even spell . . . no wonder he's on the raffia table . . .

FLORA. Now . . . Hetty left instructions for me to open this box . . .

ROSALIND. It couldn't be our 'thousandth performance' present could it?

CHARLIE. Oh nice . . . I love openin' presents . . . Where've she and Gert disappeared off to anyway?

HELEN. They've joined the Girl Guides. They've gone shopping for woggles . . .

They open it. It is full of identical dresses – hideous beige sack-like things – and matching balaclavas. CHARLIE *and* ROSALIND *put them on and sashay about.*

CHARLIE. Bloody Nora . . .

FLORA. I know beige is rather a trying colour but . . . well . . . Rayon is marvellous on the washing front . . . Anyway, they're a new idea of Hetty's . . . she thought it might give our war effort more status if we had a uniform . . . so no one could think we were just doing it for fun . . .

HELEN. For fun? Is she kidding? It's about as much fun as chewing a wasp . . .

ROSALIND. She probably just thinks if we all look the same then we'll have more pride in ourselves and that will boost morale . . .

HELEN. Hitler used the same argument in *Mein Kampf* but hey . . . Jesus, look at you, Ros! You look like a Durex on legs . . .

FLORA. Tell you what . . . let's throw caution to the wind and have sugar with our tea.

They choose places, put down blankets, plimsoll bags, etc. FLORA *takes out her knitting.* JOCELYN *is mending a costume.* ROSALIND *is polishing the swords.* CHARLIE *is scouring the 'dead and wounded' list in the paper.*

ROSALIND. Oh gosh, do you remember plimsoll bags? Even the word 'plimsoll' makes me feel nostalgic . . .

JOCELYN. Like 'tummy-button'.

ROSALIND. Or 'pinky' . . .

HELEN. It's wonderfully reassuring to realise, Rosalind, that you still have depths of superficiality as yet unplumbed . . . Has anyone got a Craven A I could possibly borrow? I'm desperate . . .

ROSALIND. Has everyone checked the list of dead and wounded? It's just I need the newspaper to wrap up the daggers . . .

FLORA. Not yet . . . give it here . . .

ROSALIND. Oh this is one for you, Charlie. 'The Modern Girl – Even though the modern girl threatens to expire at the mention of darning a man's sock, doesn't she rather love doing these same despised things for the one who can endow them with magic charm?'

FLORA. Oh dear, it never gets any less harrowing reading these lists . . . so many young lives . . .

JOCELYN *empties out her handbag to look for cigarettes.*

JOCELYN. What about 'persiflage' . . . lovely word . . . it just means waffle . . . persiflage . . . Charlie, give us a word . . .

CHARLIE. What's that Hetty one? 'Onomatopoeia'.

ROSALIND. Oh and . . . and 'Roucouler' . . . it's the French word for the noise doves make when they coo, 'roo-coo' . . .

FLORA. Isn't this fun? . . .'Primrose' . . . Come on, Helen, you must have some favourites?

HELEN. 'Scotch', 'chocolate', 'sex' . . . not necessarily in that order . . . Where the hell's my cigarette, Jocelyn?

JOCELYN. Here we are . . . !

JOCELYN *has emptied her bag to look for the cigarettes – she carries a spare set of shoes, some tiddlywinks, an alarm clock, a pepper-pot and some mustard.*

CHARLIE. What on earth have you got in your bag? Why've you got mustard?

JOCELYN. You never know when you might bump into a sausage . . . and pepper in the eye is very effective against a would-be ravisher . . .

HELEN. We should be so bloody lucky . . .

ROSALIND. I'm ravenous – hey, Jocelyn, can we borrow your Mrs Beeton and play 'fantasy meals' . . .

JOCELYN. I gave it to Ivy – I thought it might help . . .

HELEN. Are you sure you know the recipe for boiled eggs, Ivy?

IVY. 'Course I do . . . I'm just never sure how many minutes . . .

HELEN. Oh bloody hell . . .

FLORA. Can we not swear like troopers anymore, if you don't mind please? We are actually supposed to be doing a line-run to check we have *Oedipus Rex* under our belts . . .

IVY. I don't feel very well . . .

CHARLIE. I better tell you a story, then . . . Whenever we were ill, my mum'd tell us stories . . . They were always about this pet fox she said she had. But she'd change the name of the fox to whoever was ill . . . you know? My mum would say, 'I had this pet fox called Tommy or Billy or if it was me who was ill, a fox called Charlie' . . . and as you'd listen . . . you'd forget you were ill . . . 'cos you were in the story . . . you sort of were the story, if you know what I mean . . .

JOCELYN. Absolutely . . . Like you are the Fauré 'Requiem' when you listen to it . . .

IVY *disappears off to the bathroom.*

ROSALIND. Oh dear, I hope she's alright . . .

HELEN. I'll tell you a story . . . Once upon a time there were seven women and a stupid little dog who went round the country doing Shakespeare to poor little unsuspecting children . . . looking for some kind of magical fulfilment . . . until one day they realised there was no Emerald City . . .

CHARLIE. 'Ha ha ha, ho ho ho and a couple of tralalas!' I know, let's play guess the title!

FLORA. Oh good.

HELEN. Oh God . . . Alright . . .

HELEN *indicates it's a film.*

EVERYONE. A film?

HELEN *takes a drag of the cigarette blows out and runs through the smoke melodramatically.*

Casablanca? . . . *Macbeth*? *Up the Pole*?

ROSALIND. *Wizard of Oz*? *Goodbye Mister Chips*?

HELEN. Is there a village missing its idiot? In what way does that say Robert Donat or Dorothy?

IVY *returns looking pale.*

IVY. Sorroy . . .

HELEN. It was *Gone with the Wind*, actually – Scarlett O'Hara running through the burning city of Atlanta . . .

FLORA. What are you apologising for, you big silly?

IVY. Because I forgot to put the eggs on . . .

CHARLIE. No no, she wasn't running, she was in a horse-and-buggy thing . . . or was that Rhett?

HELEN. 'Frankly my dear . . .' Stupid game . . .

IVY *places the eggs in a kettle.*

IVY. I got a letter from Joseph . . . he says he wants to marry me . . .

ROSALIND. Oh Ivy . . .

IVY. But Gertrude would never agree because I've not got Jewish blood in my family. That's why we've kept everything secret from her . . . even though I told Joseph I'd learn

Hebrew and all that . . . but, oh read 'em his last letter,
Charlie . . . I'm not just being foolish, am I?

She takes it out of her bag.

CHARLIE (*reads*). 'Darling Ivy. Let me not to the marriage of
true minds admit impediments . . . I am on my knees asking
for you to do me the honour of being my wife . . . You are
my dawn, my dusk, my sun, my moon . . . you are my
homeland . . . In the Talmud it says, "Over every blade of
grass hovers an angel who whispers 'Grow grow'." . . .
You have been that angel . . . '

Everyone falls silent.

JOCELYN. You're not foolish, Ivy . . . If you want to know
about being foolish, ask me.

IVY. What do you mean?

JOCELYN. Well, I was adored once too.

IVY. 'Course you were . . .

JOCELYN. I met this young man – I never thought it would
happen for me . . . because, you know, I'd had to look after
my mother for so long, but this blessed fool asked me to
walk out with him. I didn't know a thing about sex – the
only advice my mother had ever given me was 'your shoes
come off last'.

IVY. Oh Joss.

JOCELYN. We'd had a picnic and he wanted to do a sketch
of me as a keepsake . . . I got very self-conscious but
eventually I let him and I hated it. I thought it made my
nose look strange and I got it into my head that he was
laughing at me. I got very angry . . . and I wouldn't let up.
And when he had to go he said, 'Come on, Joss – we've
only got about six minutes left together and you still want to
argue about my drawing skills' . . . And I said, 'Six minutes –
that's heaps. We've got nothing to say to each other anyway.'

IVY. What happened?

JOCELYN. Well, he stopped coming . . . and eventually I heard
he'd got engaged to another girl. And then a few months

later, his mother sent me back a book of poetry I'd lent to Jimmy . . . that was his . . . and inside – folded up – was the sketch he'd done of me. Underneath the drawing he'd written 'lovely lovely lovely' . . . You see, Ivy, you must seize the happy moments and, oh sweet gentle Lord, try to recognise them as such . . .

HELEN. This is all getting a tad gloomy . . . Let's push the boat out . . . emergency rations . . . real whisky!

She pulls out a bottle of whisky.

JOCELYN. Are you going to say yes?

IVY *smiles at her.*

FLORA. I hate to be a party-pooper but we really should be rehearsing that *Oedipus* glitch . . . Come on, the third Chorus bit with the humming and stomping.

They all hum in harmony as she speaks. It is effective but humourless.

'O healer of Helos . . . deathless Athena . . . first daughter of Zeus . . . Slay with thy golden bough Lycean who . . .' Mmmm . . . Sophocles is rather thin in the chuckle department . . . 'Slay with thy . . . oh no . . .'

The girls' stomping rhythm leads to a tap routine to 'I Got Rhythm'. They all start singing and dancing round the cloakroom . . . In the midst of it, IVY *grabs the kettle full of eggs and disappears to the bathroom. Suddenly a saxophone joins them and, as if by magic,* JOSEPH *appears.*

ROSALIND. Oh my God, look who's here . . .

They crowd about him.

JOSEPH. I have leave for one night before we fly and – abraca-dabras – I find a chauffeur.

REGGIE *appears. Whoops of delight, etc.*

REGGIE. Gosh . . . I must play chauffeur more often . . .

JOSEPH. Is my mother here?

CHARLIE. No . . . she's out. She went somewhere with Hetty and her smelly dog.

JOSEPH. Ticketyboo . . .

JOCELYN (*talking to him as if he doesn't speak English*). Not well . . . very old.

JOSEPH. Oh I'm sorry, Jocelyn.

JOCELYN. No, the dog . . . I think they took him to the vet . . .

IVY *reappears with the eggs cradled in her hands.*

IVY. Oh my goodness! How are you, Mister Panache?

REGGIE. I'm absolutely tip-top, Miss Bliss . . . though I could kill for some food and a drink . . . haven't eaten since breakfast . . .

IVY. Oh you can have my egg and there's some gooseberry jam . . . I could do you a sandwich.

REGGIE. No really, I'm fine . . .

IVY. Hey Joe . . . What you doin' here, you daft bugger?

JOSEPH *is tongue-tied.*

REGGIE. Maybe we should all step outside, girls . . .

IVY. No, it's alright . . . I mean . . . sorroy . . .

Everyone stares at her.

Um . . . Joe . . .

My bounty is as boundless as the sea,
My love as deep,
The more I give to you the more I have,
For both are infinite.

JOSEPH. That is . . . yes?

EVERYONE. YES!

Cheers. They embrace.

ROSALIND. Let's go to that dance up the road. Come on . . .

FLORA. Well, if I do come, I can't stay long . . .

REGGIE. Count me out, I'm afraid . . . back to my lodgings . . .

CHARLIE. Oh yeah, let's go . . . come on, time for a celebration . . .

ROSALIND. I should blinkin' cocoa . . . Is that right? It didn't sound very cockney . . .

CHARLIE. We'll work on it, sweetheart . . .

They go off singing 'Ivy Ivy, give me your answer do'.

HELEN. Oh God – I think I've still got some six o'clock shadow from *Julius Caesar* . . . I must just put some make-up on . . .

HELEN is desperately fiddling with her make-up – she drops it all on the floor.

ROSALIND. Are you alright – we'll catch you up. Are you alright?

HELEN. Don't fuss . . . Get me some whisky . . .

ROSALIND gets her some water and picks up the make-up. HELEN tries to draw stocking seams with an eyebrow pencil.

Oh God, where's my lipstick? . . . There are going to be men there . . . I've got to look my best . . . Draw me some stocking seams, for God's sake, I'm too shaky . . . Oh Jesus, I need someone to make me feel like a woman again. Where is the whisky, you idiot? . . .

She hands back the glass. ROSALIND tries to draw stocking seams on the back of HELEN's legs.

ROSALIND. Don't you think you've had enough to drink?

HELEN. Oh shut up, you're not my mother . . . My life has been unspeakable. I deserve to drink. Anyway, it's very healing . . . Jesus, I don't know why I'm talking to you. What would you understand about women's needs . . . you're a . . . a prepubescent refrigerator . . .

CHARLIE shouts for them to 'come on'.

(Pocketing the whisky bottle.) How do I look?

ROSALIND (*bitterly*). Like a star . . .

They exit, turning out the lights.

Late-night wireless. Light comes up.

FLORA in a nighty brings on a tray of bread and jam.
GERTRUDE comes in.

GERTRUDE. Ich bin so müde, ich muss mich irgendwo
hinlegen, wo ich nicht gestört werde . . . [I am so tired,
I must lie down where I won't be disturbed . . .]

She exits into the school. FLORA returns and turns off the
wireless. She kneels down and says a short prayer. HETTY
comes in wearing one of the beige dresses and a balaclava.

HETTY. Where on earth is everyone?

FLORA. They must have gone for a walk . . . My, doesn't
beige look fetching on you? . . . How is everything? What
did the vet say?

HETTY looks away and takes the dog-lead out of her
pocket.

Oh Lor', Hetty, you didn't . . . was it . . . oh Hetty, I'm
sorry . . . 'there's a great spirit gone' . . .

HETTY. No, please don't be nice to me or I'll break down . . .

GERTRUDE starts to play in the distance. FLORA pours
some tea.

FLORA. Would you like something to eat? Don't worry, that's
not being nice . . . Ivy was on cooking duty . . . Is that
Gertrude?

HETTY. She's in one of her grievings . . . It'll be Beethoven,
I imagine . . .

HETTY picks up the list of dead and wounded and reads it
in silence.

So much death . . . Someone . . . I can't remember who . . .
said that we should say to each child, 'You are a marvel.
What a wonder you are – your eyes, your cunning fingers,
the way you move. You might become a Beethoven, a

Michelangelo, a Shakespeare. You have the capacity for
anything . . . And so, when you grow up, can you then harm
another who is, like you, a marvel?' Oh God, Flora, sometimes
I'm frightened it's just not worth it . . . dragging you all about
in appalling conditions . . . working ludicrous hours . . .

FLORA. Nonsense . . . why even today I was reading a letter
from a dear little marvel who thought we were worth much
more than fivepence . . . she thought we were worth at least
sixpence . . .

They both laugh.

You're allowed not to be strong all the time, you know,
Hetty . . . let me take care of you for five minutes . . .

HETTY (*putting away the lead*). Sometimes you wish you'd
never allowed yourself to feel so much . . .

HETTY *falls silent.* GERTRUDE *plays Brahms in the
distance.* FLORA *lights a cigarette and hands it to* HETTY.

FLORA. The terrible thing about pets is that the ones you
absolutely loathe seem to live forever . . .

HETTY *pulls back the blackout on the window. The light of
the full moon comes through .*

HETTY. What a strange day . . . twilight and darkening . . .
and then luminous . . . Why is it women who are made mad
by the moon?

FLORA. Women, Irish wolves and apparently penguins . . .

HETTY. That's right . . . You've always had a problem with
full moons and I've never been very sympathetic . . . I'm
sorry, is it one of your silly superstitions?

FLORA. No . . . no . . . although it is possibly rather silly . . .
It has a story . . . I don't know why I've never told you
before . . .

FLORA *gets some bread and the jam and makes
sandwiches as she talks.*

You see, when my mother died, we went to live with my
grandmother on a house by a lake . . . And for my little

brother Toby and I, it was . . . well, it was a Wonderland because, you see, my father was almost never there . . . and he wasn't a very nice man . . . he wasn't kind to Toby . . . and Toby was such a gentle soul, he couldn't . . . you don't really want to hear all this . . .

HETTY. Yes I do . . . just a scrape of margarine . . .

FLORA. Well, we used to play make-believe in the woods . . . we'd pretend to be Babushka and Marushka, the Elfin king and queen, having banquets and things . . . And sometimes we'd lie back in the grass and Toby would say, 'Listen Marushka – I can hear the flowers growing' . . . He loved flowers . . . he was always picking them for everyone . . . you'd wake up and there was a little bunch of primroses on the pillow . . . and he was always asking me impossible questions . . . 'What's sky?' And I'd say, 'It's where heaven is . . .' and he'd say, 'What's it like to die?' . . . and it was awkward, you know, I mean I didn't have the answers – and I'd say, 'It's like going home – to our real home where Mumma is . . . and God' . . . And he'd say, 'Will God like me as I am?' And I said, 'Yes Toby, he'll like you very much.' Honestly, Hetty, I'll tell you another time . . .

HETTY. Please, I want you to go on . . . just one round . . . thanks.

FLORA. Well, years went by and Toby was sent to a boarding school because my father said he needed toughening up and he hated it . . . and my father would thrash him because his report would say he was a coward on the rugby field, and still a mother's boy . . . and so on . . . and he'd come into my bed – you see, he was terrified of the dark – and he'd cry into my hair and he'd say, 'Oh Flora, something's not right with me . . . Why am I wrong?'

And then when he was fourteen . . . It was one winter evening, my father had gone out and we had the wonderful sense of being able to breathe again that we always had . . . and Toby said he had a surprise for me and I was to come when he called . . . he was in our mother's old room which we were forbidden from ever entering and so I knew it was something special . . . when I opened the door, the curtains were shut and there was no one there . . . just lots of candles placed about the room . . . and the gramophone was on . . . playing the silliest song that our mother simply loved about a little speckly hen . . . and then . . . the curtains opened and he stepped forward and . . . and he had reddened his lips and his cheeks . . . and he looked so beautiful . . . so like our mother . . . and he was wearing her ivory-lace dressing gown and when he looked in the mirror, he laughed . . . you know, that wonderful infectious laugh people have when they are really happy . . . and we danced round and round the room and we were . . . shimmering . . .

And then suddenly the door opened and my father was standing there . . . and I've never seen anyone so angry . . . And he grabbed Toby and he said, 'How dare you – how dare you bring shame on the memory of your mother – don't you ever – don't you ever – no son of mine will be a . . .' And he used terrible words . . . I don't have to tell you. And I was begging him, saying, 'Daddy, stop it . . . stop it, Daddy' – and finally he said he was sending him to an army school and if that didn't make a man of him . . .

And Toby didn't say anything . . . he just stared at him . . . And all the time this silly song was still playing about a speckly hen . . . but it had slowed right down . . . which should have been so funny . . .

That night I said my prayers . . . and I begged God to smite down my father and to take him out of our lives . . . and then I thought I heard a noise outside and so I went to the window . . . it was a beautiful ice-cold night with a full moon . . . and still . . . so still . . . as if the world was holding its breath . . . Toby was standing on the frozen lake in the moonlight . . . he was completely naked . . . and I called to him . . . I begged him to come in and I told him how much I loved him and how I would hug away his loneliness . . . And he just looked at me so calmly and he said, 'Marushka . . . Marushka . . . I'm going home' . . . And there was a sound . . . you know, the sound the ice makes when it cracks . . . only it wasn't the ice . . . he'd taken my father's army gun and he'd shot himself . . .

I never wanted children after that . . . And I know it's silly but I always felt that if only there hadn't been that full moon he wouldn't have done it . . . because it would have been dark . . . and he was always so frightened of the dark . . .

HETTY. Well thank you, Flora, that's really cheered me up . . .

FLORA. Oh dear – no, all I mean is that *in spite of* everything, I do believe in God and I think the fact that we have loved, well, that somehow testifies to . . . Sorry, I've been a bit waffly . . . persiflage . . .

HETTY. Bless you, Flora . . . You're a very dear friend . . . But who knows? Perhaps God didn't create us . . . perhaps *because of* everything, we created God . . . as the most necessary make-believe of all . . .

FLORA. Do you remember that moment at the very end of *Pilgrim's Progress* as he steps into the river? 'And all the trumpets sounded for him on the other side.'

FLORA *breaks down.*

Big-band sound. High-energy dancing. All the girls are dancing and are extremely drunk. BERT *appears at the microphone.*

BERT. The Blackout Stroll. You ladies called 'wallflowers' – fated to sit out all the dances because perhaps your face isn't your future or your figure isn't the cuddly kind – here's your chance to dance the latest step. And your godsend . . . when the lights go out, you change partners in the dark . . .

BERT *sings.* HELEN *joins him and drunkenly sings along.*

Lights go out. HELEN *and* BERT *kissing drunkenly, watched in disgust by* ROSALIND.

More song. Lights go out. JOSEPH *and* IVY *slow-dance.*

JOSEPH.
When I have you dance, I would wish you a wave of the sea
That you might ever do nothing but that
Move still, still so,
And own no other function.

They continue to turn slowly and kiss tenderly as the light fades . . .

ROSALIND *and* CHARLIE *are stumbling back into the peg room.*

CHARLIE. What was that word for when doves coo?

ROSALIND. 'Roucouler' . . . roo-coo roo-coo . . . onomatopoeia.

CHARLIE. Mmm . . .

They kiss on the lips very tenderly.

(*Whispering.*) Thy lips are warm . . .

ROSALIND. We mustn't . . . It's . . .

CHARLIE *magically extracts a bunch of paper flowers from behind* ROSALIND*'s ear.*

CHARLIE. Why? How can it be alright to kiss as characters in front of lots of strangers but not in private . . .

ROSALIND. I don't know . . . it's not natural . . .

CHARLIE. Why not? Who made that decision? Why should we feel ashamed for loving each other? It seems natural to me . . . it seems lovely and gentle and . . . I'm not going to be ashamed . . .

ROSALIND. When the war's over, things won't be so bonkers . . .

CHARLIE. How can we possibly change back? The war's been the best thing that ever happened to us . . . Don't change . . . please don't change . . . (*They kiss.*)

They pull apart as they hear the others arriving. There is a crash from beyond the cloakroom.

IVY (*offstage*). Ooops . . . Sorroy!

They are whispering drunkenly, lots of shushing, as they enter.

I hope Joe and Mister Pelmet were allowed back in the guesthouse . . . they was ever so . . . merry . . . ooh I'm so weary, I've come over all unnecessary . . .

She lies down.

ROSALIND. Hey Jocelyn . . . saw you dancing with that funny chap . . . the vicar . . .

JOCELYN. Bless him . . . He'd had an arm amputated . . .

ROSALIND. What a shame . . .

HELEN. Hey, don't mock it . . . funny one-armed vicars don't grow on trees you know . . .

ROSALIND. Shhh . . .

HELEN. Don't shush me, there's nobody bloody here . . . No, all I'm saying is . . . We should jettison Shakespeare . . . overboard with him . . . 'TTFN'.

JOCELYN. The trick with Shakespeare is only to play kings and queens – you never have to carry props and you always get a chair . . .

FLORA *appears.* IVY *goes to the bathroom.*

FLORA. Shhh, you must all go to sleep . . .

CHARLIE. Miss Oak'll have us for dereliction of duty . . .

ROSALIND. Ooh scary scary.

FLORA. Stop it all of you . . . no more talking . . .

HELEN. Oh yeah, I know . . . thanks Flora . . . 'Rest, rest, perturbed spirit' – well no, I was born without brakes . . .

FLORA. I beg you to stop . . .

HELEN. No . . . no, listen Flora . . . we've travelled ten thousand miles around Britain and done one thousand performances of thirty-five plays – just seven of us – SEVEN – playing an obscenely ludicrous number of parts – driven by what? Who is she? Who does she think she is? Mrs Miniver?

FLORA. This is the drink talking . . .

HELEN *takes* HETTY*'s trench coat and parades in it.*

HELEN. 'Why, man, she doth bestride the narrow world like a Colossus' . . . but, you see, inside this ridiculous dog-

stinking coat . . . there hides the true Hetty Oak – a
menopausal dwarf . . .

The beam of a bright torchlight hits them.

HETTY. Nobody's hiding anywhere . . . but we have three
shows here tomorrow and if even one of you isn't up to the
task, you will be jeopardising our whole enterprise and
bringing down not simply the morale of this company but
the morale of the people of Britain. We do have a duty to
perform . . . this is your war effort . . . Now goodnight, all
of you . . .

HELEN. Oh come on, Mister Churchill. Even soldiers get . . .
compassionate leave or whatever . . . I mean, thanks a lot
but we're dying here . . .

HETTY. No . . . Christ, how dare you? . . . Of course you're
not . . . Young boys are lying bleeding in the mud . . .
brilliant musicians and poets are hanging like scarecrows
on barbed wire so that you can go galavanting off and drink
yourself stupid and make fools of yourselves . . . You want
sympathy? You'll find it in the dictionary between shit and
syphilis . . .

HELEN. Exactly . . . War doesn't give a shit about Artists . . .

HETTY. Oh for God's sake, Helen, grow up . . .

HELEN. Why the hell should I? What are you going to do . . .
court-martial me? If you dismiss me, you don't just get rid
of one mutinous foot soldier . . . oh no . . . I take with me
over two hundred characters . . . I'm riddled with
characters.

HETTY. May I speak . . .

HELEN. No . . . you can shut up for once in your life . . . Shut
up!

ROSALIND. Mummy . . .

HELEN. For Christ's sake, we're women . . . but you need us
to be men on and off the stage . . . because it terrifies you . . .
because when we consort with real men . . . real men . . .
it's like bullet-wounds in your side because you can't

control us any more . . . we're beyond the barbed-wire fence . . . (*She mimes a gun.*) Bham bham . . . because what do you know about how we feel? You know nothing about feelings, parading about in your stupid soldier coat. You've never been a woman – You've always been a man . . .

There is a terrifying silence.

HETTY. This coat isn't actually mine . . . it belonged to my father . . . who I loved . . . and I wear it constantly because when he was killed, it was the only way I could find of keeping him alive . . . And if in any other way you're interested in my female credentials . . . I have . . . I have a . . . Oh what does it matter? . . . Now I believe your other point was has this all been a waste of time? Well, has it? I don't think so when I look out at all those children's faces . . . But you're probably right – I've been taking refuge in fiction . . . I'm sorry . . . truly I am . . . so let's go home . . .

HETTY *leaves.*

HELEN. Has anyone got a cigarette I could borrow?

The lights fade down until there is only HETTY *sitting on a hamper, writing.*

HETTY (*reads*). 'Now the sun is finally up . . . I've packed everything and, when I have put this in the post, I'll be leaving . . . So, my darling, it's all over . . . let be . . . '

CHARLIE, FLORA *and* JOCELYN *arrive, looking at each other helplessly as they load all the things together.* FLORA *has a tray of tea and some biscuits.*

FLORA. I made a nice cup of tea for everyone and everyone's disappeared.

HETTY. Since there's no more company, they can do what they please . . .

CHARLIE. Ros went to try to find black pudding for breakfast . . . It is your favourite, isn't it, Miss Oak?

HETTY. That's very kind but I really must be on my way . . . You just need to load up and then the rest of you can go in Caprice. Remember to check her tyres, Charlie . . .

CHARLIE. At least have a cup of tea before you go . . .

FLORA. Oh Hetty, this is ridiculous, please re-consider . . .

HETTY. You're very sweet, Flora, but I think it's time everyone went back to their families and got on with their lives . . .

FLORA. This company is my family . . .

HETTY. Oh Flora, please . . .

CHARLIE. Oh Miss Oak, please don't mess it all up . . . When I left school they said, if I was lucky I'd get a job in a shop . . . and, I mean, it was the same for all of us . . . we were nothing . . . and you made me believe I didn't have to be that . . . This company's been the best thing that ever happened to me . . . Oh can't we just all make up? Can I take one of them biscuits?

She tucks in to the biscuits.

JOCELYN. Oh Lord, are we all meant to be saying something inspirational? . . . I'm a batty old lady, as you all know . . . so old in fact that one of the children yesterday asked me if I knew Shakespeare! I said we were on very good terms . . . Oh don't go, Hetty . . .

HETTY. Very kind but honestly . . .

FLORA. Do have a shortbread finger, Hetty – they're McVities . . .

HELEN *and* ROSALIND *arrive with a black pudding.*

HELEN. Look what we found for breakfast! I have in my hand a black pudding – and I am not afraid to use it! I, of course, will be eating humble pie . . . Why are you all packed up? Oh no, this is all my fault . . . mea unilaterally culpa. Has anyone got an aspirin I could borrow?

HETTY. Honestly, it's for the best . . . if someone could just refund this school for today's cancelled show, I'll sort out the rest . . .

IVY *appears.*

IVY. Miss Oak . . . I can't stay in the troupe . . .

HETTY. Join the club.

FLORA. Good heavens, Ivy – why ever not?

IVY. How can I play loads of blokes when I'm pregnant?

ROSALIND. Oh you poor thing . . . that's why you rushed off to the . . .

FLORA. Oh Ivy, you should have waited . . . till you were married . . .

IVY. Sorroy . . .

IVY *breaks down in floods of tears.*

HETTY. Is it Joseph's?

IVY. Yes.

HETTY. Do you love him?

IVY. Yes.

HETTY. Well, then I think that's splendid.

IVY. I thought you'd be really vexed.

HETTY. Why?

IVY. Because I'm messing everything up and we're not married even though we are engaged and I'm not Jewish . . .

HETTY. How can having a baby be messing up anything? And I'm certain God won't give a tuppenny-hoot if you're Jewish or not . . . This baby's a gift that no one can take away from you . . . never never never . . . We'll sort things out . . . don't you worry, my lamb . . .

IVY. But it's such a terrible time to bring a baby into the world . . .

HETTY. No . . . it's always a wonderful time to bring a baby into the world . . .

IVY. You don't believe that . . .

HETTY. I most certainly do . . .

IVY. Otherwise why didn't you ever have children?

HETTY. But I did . . . I . . . I did have a baby . . . But you see, Ivy, mine wasn't a love-child . . . It wasn't conceived in love . . . it was conceived in . . . in hate, I'm afraid . . . and when it was born, I was so . . . I didn't even want to hold . . . I was . . . For a very long time I didn't think I could ever forgive the man . . . forgive all men, I suppose . . . because yes, they are stronger than us but no, I am not a man and I have no desire to be one . . . And anyway, the theory isn't necessarily the same as the reality because my child came and found me . . . not long before the war broke out he came and found me . . . and we've been getting to know each other. He's called Crispian Wilson . . . and I think he's pretty special . . . but of course every mother thinks that don't they, Helen? So you see, out of the worst thing that ever happened to me came the best thing . . .

IVY. Will we get to meet him?

HETTY. I do hope so. At the moment he's somewhere in France . . . he's sitting in the mud with a gun in his lap because he's a twenty-year-old boy and twenty-year-old boys haven't got a choice . . . But he knows all about our exploits . . . and he's always hungry for the next instalment . . .

HELEN. Perhaps you could skip the most recent one . . .

HETTY. Of course he'll be disappointed that things haven't worked out because I think both he and I want to believe the same thing . . . that there is something worth fighting for . . .

IVY. But that's why I don't want to mess everything up because I think we really have been doing something good for people . . . that stops them thinkin' that life's just the bad stuff . . .

HETTY. You're quite right, Ivy . . . In war we're all too horribly aware of the bad stuff . . . and that is why we women can make a difference – if only in our little way – because when we connect with our great writers and with our audience and with each other . . . that collective imagination . . . why, then we're promoting the good stuff. All that's required from us – is that we reawaken people's faith in humanity. Us – Charlie, Flora, Gertrude, Jocelyn, Rosalind, you . . . me . . . Helen.

She wipes IVY*'s face with her hanky.*

Anyway, you can play all the fat blokes like Falstaff . . .

IVY. I could do all the cooking . . .

ALL. No, no need for that . . . We'll do it.

HETTY. Come on, we need to get this stuff back inside . . .
What are we doing today?

JOCELYN. *Much Ado About Nothing*!

HETTY. Absolutely . . .

IVY. I wish you were my mum . . . I mean, you're ever so
much nicer than you seem . . .

HETTY. Thank you . . .

IVY. You'd actually make someone a lovely wife . . . you're so
wise an' all that . . .

HETTY. Mmmm . . . It is not necessarily a virtue men find
attractive. People often ask why I never married – they
never stop to think perhaps no one ever asked me . . .

HELEN. As Oscar Wilde so memorably said . . . No, sorry . . .
can't remember . . .

HETTY. 'In married life, three's company and two none . . .'
Now Ivy, I believe you have some good news to share with
Joseph . . . We'll set up inside while you two can cook the
breakfast . . . I gather we're having a black pudding . . .

They all exit except HELEN *and* ROSALIND.

HELEN. My! What dark horses they all are! Am I alone in
feeling we've been Hetty'd again? Mind you, she certainly
gets my nomination for the 'Mary of Nazareth Suffering
Motherhood' Award.

ROSALIND. Stop it . . . Mummy, you're a fine one to talk . . .
God, I wish I had been adopted . . .

HELEN. How dare you?

ROSALIND. How dare *you*? . . . You are such a hypocrite . . .
I'm going to find Charlie . . .

HELEN. God, what a woundingly unkind thing to say, Ros . . .
I may be fond of a little 'panache' . . . but that's not
hypocrisy . . . it's wit . . .

ROSALIND. When did you care about kind? You despise nice
and kind . . .

HELEN. Oh for God's sake, Ros, listen . . .

ROSALIND. No, you listen to me for once. You've spent your
whole life cowering behind some stupid notion that you
don't have to behave because you're witty or because you
are a 'star' or at least you were . . . and therefore better
than other people . . . You know that's rubbish . . . you know
that . . . the only thing special about stars is that they're
completely indifferent to everyone and everything that
doesn't centre on them . . . You're just a middle-aged
woman who pretends to be someone else for a living, that's
all . . . Good God . . . a lifetime of you judging me? I tried
everything to make you love me . . . but I was always
jostling for affection somewhere between the mirror and
your whisky tumbler . . .

HELEN. Why are you saying all this?

ROSALIND. Because you no longer frighten me . . . there is a
world elsewhere . . .

She goes to leave.

HELEN. Oh Ros . . . now you're frightening me . . . stop,
please, being horrid.

ROSALIND. Why the hell should I?

HELEN. Because I don't know how to cook this enormous
sausage . . . no, sorry . . . Come back here and we'll make
up . . . come on, Snow White.

ROSALIND. No, you said I have no passion. I feel but you
don't know what I feel . . . I dream but you don't know what
I dream . . . and you dare say where's the woman in me?
Anyway, you're more than sufficient for the both of us . . .
and I don't care because after living with you and Daddy . . .
well, if that's marriage then I don't want to have anything

to do with it . . . and I will never have children if it means
making them as miserable as you have made me . . .

HELEN. Please Rossy, I'm not arguing . . . look . . . let me
comb your hair . . . we're always friends when I comb your
hair . . .

ROSALIND. Stop this . . . It's too late to play Mummy . . .

HELEN. Of course it is . . . you're right . . . I'm tired of being
vile . . . Oh God, I've got a headache . . . Am I as heartless
as you say? Am I capable of loving anyone? I loved my
mother . . . I loved her . . . infinitely . . . and when she
died . . . I couldn't bear it and . . . and I think I panicked
and all the love . . . flew away . . . like a bird had flown
out of my heart . . . But then you came along . . . beautiful
you . . . and you allowed me to believe that death wasn't
the end . . .

ROSALIND. Being a daughter means having a separate
identity, not being your mother's understudy.

HELEN. If it's any compensation, I'm not sure if I've ever
liked myself very much. I was always hoping I'd stumble
across a character that I'd like better than me . . . and then
I'd borrow it . . . and . . . and we'd all be a happy family . . .
instead of which, you got . . . and maybe I did . . . maybe
I started banishing everything and everyone before they
banished me . . . Is that what's happened? That I've made
absolutely certain you'd never care about me so much, you
couldn't bear losing me? Well, you have to admit I've made
a success of that . . . Oh God, this is so hard . . . Look, I
promise I will never come between you and the possibility
of love ever again . . . and I will try to stop drinking . . .

ROSALIND. Let's shake on it.

They shake hands.

HELEN. Oh dear, this is all getting very King Lear and
Cordelia . . . I couldn't possibly . . . ?

ROSALIND. I don't smoke . . .

HELEN. Of course you don't. Quite right too. Another area in
which you absolutely should not follow my example. You

know when you were a little girl I introduced you to George Bernard Shaw . . . 'This,' I said proudly, 'is Mister Bernard Shaw. He is one of our greatest writers.' And you looked at him with your little eyes full of wonder and said, 'Really? Can you do "w"s?'

IVY *appears behind* JOSEPH *and* GERTRUDE *arguing furiously in German.*

JOSEPH. Aber ich liebe sie! [But I love her!]

GERTRUDE. Das ist unmöglich, sie ist keine Jüdin. [That's impossible, she is no Jew.]

JOSEPH. Das ist mir gleich! Ich werde sie trotzdem heiraten. [That doesn't matter, I will marry her anyway.]

IVY. What's happened? Joe, what's the matter?

ROSALIND. What is it, Gertrude?

HELEN. Jesus, what's happened now?

JOSEPH. She is saying she cannot give her blessing to our marriage . . . that our religion will not allow it . . . But it doesn't matter, Ivy . . . because you are my faith . . .

He takes her face in his hands.

IVY. But you must tell her it's alright, Joe, because Miss Oak says God doesn't mind if we're not the same religion . . . He loves everyone as long as they're good . . . and He'll love the baby whatever . . .

GERTRUDE *and* JOSEPH *look at her.*

GERTRUDE. Das Kind? [The baby?]

GERTRUDE *rushes off and* IVY, HELEN *and* ROSALIND *follow.*

REGGIE (*who has arrived just after* JOSEPH *and* IVY) *walks forward and puts his arm around a distraught* JOSEPH.

REGGIE. . . . I was never lucky enough to start a family – I never had that honour – so what do I know about these things? – I'm a . . . an observer, a looker-on. But I'm a great

believer in Time. I've always found Time to be a
tremendous ally.

I remember watching some fishermen trying to row home
from their trawler – the wind and the tide were against them
– it was bitterly cold . . . Every time I looked, they seemed
to be further back than before and I thought, 'Well – they'll
never get home, they'll be . . .' But they did. Four strokes
forward, three strokes back. But they got there . . . I'm not
sure if that helps but . . . Time . . . Anyway, cheer up old
thing and . . . congratulations . . .

*Piano and saxophone music. Everybody emerges in top hats
and tails.* IVY *in a spotlight sings a ballad of the period
(e.g., Noël Coward's 'If Love Were All') as* HETTY *reads.*

HETTY (*reads*). 'My darling boy. I hardly dare let myself
think that this dreadful war is coming to an end and you
will be home. But it is and you will . . .

*The others hum to the music and do a discreet dance
routine.*

We've all now seen those harrowing photographs of the
death camps . . . and dear God . . . how will the Jewish
race ever be able to forget . . . or forgive? . . . Gertrude
has a husband missing . . . but even all this is no excuse
for her treatment of Ivy which is utterly senseless. And
yet Ivy is kinder than ever . . . Well, perhaps when the baby
is born . . . '

*The lights fade as the piano continues and changes into a
different tune. When the lights come up,* IVY *is now heavily
pregnant in one of the (specially adapted) beige frocks.
Others are in overcoats and are freezing.* FLORA *has the
wings and a needle and thread.* GERTRUDE *plays piano to
underscore and totally ignores* IVY.

HETTY (Prospero). You'd be king o' the isle, sirrah?

CHARLIE (Stephano). I should have been a sore one, then.

FLORA (Alonso, *pointing to* JOCELYN *as Caliban*). This is a
strange thing as e'er I looked on.

HETTY (Prospero). Go, sirrah, to my cell;
Take with you your companions.

JOCELYN (Caliban). Ay that I will; and I'll be wise hereafter . . .

CHARLIE *and* JOCELYN *exit stage-right.*

HETTY (Prospero). Sir, I invite you . . . (*Out of character.*)
Stage-right? No, get off stage-left . . . how many more
times! There will be hardly any space on that side . . . it's
where they keep the milking-machine . . .

They all rush back and exit stage-left. GERTRUDE *coughs.*
FLORA *finishes mending the wings and fits them on* IVY.

CHARLIE. Oh right . . . So here you're talking the decrepit
toilet as opposed to the decrepit kitchen . . .

JOCELYN. I've put the kettle on . . .

IVY. I'm ever so parched . . . And you sound like you need a
cup of something, Mrs Rosenbaum . . . will I get you one?

HETTY. In a minute, Ivy . . . (Prospero.) Sir, I invite you to
my poor cell . . .

FLORA. By the by, the Scouts will be needing the hut in half
an hour . . .

HETTY. Alright, cut cue to cue. (Prospero.) My Ariel, chick,
That is thy charge. Then to the elements
Be free, and fare thou well . . .

IVY *puts a shawl round* GERTRUDE'*s shoulders. She
ignores her.* IVY *exits stage-left, singing and spinning with
clownish mischief. Everyone laughs.*

(*Out of character.*) We're achieving the disbelief . . . it's the
willing suspension that's missing from the equation . . .

*Over the sound of the singing is another sound: a V-1
(doodle-bug). It stops. There is an enormous explosion and
the terrible sound of splintering glass. They all instinctively
throw themselves down.* GERTRUDE *starts praying.*

Christ!

GERTRUDE. I'ay-lo min kol bir-ho-so v'shee-ro-so tush-b'ho
   so v'ne-heh-mo-so da-a-mee-ron b'ol-mo. [Blessed be He,
   beyond all the blessings and hymns, praises and
   consolations that are ever spoken in the world; and say,
   Amen.]

CHARLIE. Oh my God. Is anyone hurt? Ros?

ROSALIND. Oh Charlie, that was so close . . .

They crawl into each other's arms. Sirens start to wail.

FLORA. Dear God, we're alive . . . It must have hit the waste-
   land at the back . . .

HELEN. There may be more . . . Where's Ivy, for God's sake?

JOCELYN. Didn't she go to get Gertrude a cup of tea? . . . Oh
   my Lord!

   IVY *comes back on. Her wings are askew and her dress is
   dusty.*

HETTY. Oh thank God . . . you're alright . . .

HELEN. Well done, kid . . .

JOCELYN. D'you know the funniest thing is I suddenly got
   hiccoughs when . . .

IVY. Y'hay sh'lo-mo ra-bo min sh'ma-yo V'ha-yeem. [May
   there be abundant peace from heaven.]

   GERTRUDE *looks up at her in astonishment. As she recites
   the prayer, blood starts to seep through the wings. As the
   women look on in horror,* IVY *collapses. Everyone, except*
   GERTRUDE *who is in shock, instinctively works as a team
   shouting and talking over each other . . .*

ROSALIND. I'll fetch a doctor or . . . or something . . .

FLORA. Shall we prop her head up . . . oh what do we do? . . .

CHARLIE. I'm just lifting your head up, babe . . . that's right . . .
   hey beauty-girl . . .

JOCELYN. Is there a phone anywhere?

HETTY. Good . . . yes . . . I'll look here . . . you go . . .

HELEN. There you go, sweetheart . . . It's going to be just
fine . . .

CHARLIE *kneels beside her, holding her hand.*

CHARLIE. Hey, I never did tell you my story, did I? . . . Well,
anyway, I once had a fox called Ivy . . . well, believe it
or not . . . she lived with us in an old railway carriage . . .
and . . .

IVY *lets out a loud cry.*

It's alright to cry, baby lamb, we're all family . . . oh God, I'm
no good at telling stories . . . Why's there all this blood . . . ?

HELEN. Oh sweet Jesus.

JOCELYN. We're all here, poppet . . . just hold on . . .

ROSALIND *is banging on the door.*

ROSALIND. Something's blocking the door.

A few go to help. IVY *cries out.* GERTRUDE *goes to her.*

I need everyone!

All go but GERTRUDE. IVY *puts out her hand which is
covered in blood and* GERTRUDE *grasps it and kisses it.*

GERTRUDE. Herr Gott, verzeihe mir . . . God, forgive me . . .
forgive me, Ivy . . .

IVY. No need . . . oh Gertrude . . . the baby . . . don't let our
baby die . . . (*Whispers.*) . . . Sorroy . . .

The others return. CHARLIE *pushes* GERTRUDE *out the
way.*

CHARLIE. Happy with what you've done, you stupid bloody
German . . . you stupid racialist Jew.

HETTY. It's no good, it won't budge.

GERTRUDE. Flora – hot water and soap, I must wash my
hands . . . Jocelyn – towels and linen for bandages . . .
Helen – keep her warm with coat . . . Charlie – keep talking
to her . . . don't let her let go . . .

CHARLIE. What do you know about anything, you're not a bloody doctor . . .

GERTRUDE. I'm a mother . . . my husband is a doctor . . .

HELEN. She's going awfully still . . . wake up, darling . . .

GERTRUDE. Come, Ivy . . . awake for the baby . . .

JOCELYN. Her eyes aren't opening . . .

GERTRUDE. She mustn't go to sleep . . . Charlie . . . your story . . .

CHARLIE. I can't . . .

HETTY. So one day the fox disappeared and Charlie's mother found her under the bed and said, 'Don't you ever give me a fright like that, you silly old thing.'

JOCELYN. . . . Stay with us, poppet . . .

HETTY. It's alright, we're all here, we're all here for you, my lamb . . .

GERTRUDE. She's stopped breathing . . .

CHARLIE. She's not breathing, what do we do . . . ?

ROSALIND. Ivy, wake up . . . you must wake up . . . oh God, please let a miracle happen . . .

JOCELYN. Come on, darling . . . wake up, angel . . .

GERTRUDE *pulls a feather from the wings and puts it on her lips. Nothing.* GERTRUDE *disappears.*

GERTRUDE. She's gone . . .

HELEN. Oh Jesus . . . let there be a heaven . . .

CHARLIE. Oh no, it can't be true . . . no, you must be wrong . . .

ROSALIND. Ivy . . . come on . . . come back . . .

JOCELYN. Fly away, little bird . . .

HETTY *cradles her in her arms and whispers to her.* GERTRUDE *returns. She pours hot water from the kettle over a kitchen knife.*

CHARLIE. What are you doing . . . she's mad . . . Don't you touch her or I'll kill you . . .

GERTRUDE. We will deliver baby now.

HELEN. We have to try to save the baby.

ROSALIND. Oh please God.

CHARLIE. Jesus, no . . .

HETTY. It's the only chance . . .

GERTRUDE kneels beside IVY as if in prayer. Blackout.

A deafening cacophony of war-sounds – planes, bombs, sirens, marching soldiers, etc. The costume rails spin as fragments of dialogue are shouted out.

JOCELYN. And that was the end.

ROSALIND. No . . . no . . . it wasn't.

HELEN. It should have been.

CHARLIE. Why didn't we stop?

ROSALIND. Because we couldn't stop just because peace had broken out . . .

FLORA. Because we still had a duty to perform.

HETTY. Because we had to go for the final push . . .

The sound changes to waves and crying seagulls as the stage is cleared to an empty space encircled by the rails draped in white cloths.

JOCELYN. Possibly not our finest hour.

FLORA. Oh dear, that's right . . . everyone was desperate to see Laurence Olivier's splendid film . . .

JOCELYN. But some unfortunate people didn't have a picture house . . .

ROSALIND. So we were the next best thing.

CHARLIE. Unfortunately.

JOCELYN. VE Day.

ROSALIND. *Henry V.*

HELEN. The Isle of Skye . . . And given our luck, we still
seemed incapable of avoiding every kind of backstage
disaster since the tortoise fell on the head of Aeschylus . . .

JOCELYN. What was it this time?

Everyone disappears except FLORA.

FLORA. All our *Henry* props and costumes got mislaid in
transit . . . and cancellation stared us in the face.

HETTY *makes a determined entrance.*

HETTY. Cancel? Don't talk such tommyrot.

FLORA. But I've just been to the quay again and all they've
rescued were those beards.

HETTY. The readiness is all.

FLORA. But what on earth can we do?

HETTY. We improvise.

FLORA. Quite right.

HETTY. I have commandeered some distinctively English garb
from the village and am now going in search of something
that says 'French'. The rest of the gang are in the beach
huts over there getting changed.

FLORA. Oh Hetty, what a hoot . . . Oh dear, I am going to
miss all this.

HETTY. As the wonderful Mister T.S. Eliot says, 'In the end is
our beginning.' We'll be back.

*She leaves as the other women arrive on the beach in
cricket clothes and beards –* CHARLIE *and* ROSALIND
laughing hysterically.

CHARLIE. Oy!

ROSALIND *and* HELEN. Oy!

JOCELYN. Oy! Hey Mister, how are you?

CHARLIE. What do we look like? What exactly happened?

FLORA. You know that little car-ferry thing just for cars and stuff? Well, it capsized . . . I mean, it lurched or something . . .

ROSALIND. No, I know it's not funny but . . . I mean it's awful . . . but it is quite funny . . .

JOCELYN. Full fathom five poor Caprice lies.

HELEN. Which means we are sans props, sans clothes, sans lights, sans everything.

FLORA. Except the indomitable spirit of the Artemis Players . . . The show must go on . . . Who knows, it might be the new look! I'll just pop into a beach hut . . . Nil desperandum everyone . . .

She exits. They are in hysterics again.

HELEN. Funny? Absolutely yes . . . but then again, no . . . We owe it to them and ourselves to go for this final push . . . Richardson, Gielgud . . . all our great actors are back in the West End . . . bastards . . . our time is coming to a close . . . But . . . But . . . in our small way as the Queen so rightly said, 'We have inscribed our names indelibly on the national role of honour.' That's the end of my speech . . . feel free to applaud . . .

JOCELYN. Remind me why we're doing it on the beach . . .

ROSALIND. Earth, fire, water, air.

HELEN. . . . perfect theatre space . . .

CHARLIE. We shall act upon the beaches . . . we shall act upon the seas . . . These wellies are bloomin' ginormous . . .

ROSALIND. They're all ginormous and they stink of fish . . . I don't think it's what Shakespeare intended for Princess Katherine . . .

GERTRUDE *and* REGGIE *appear with a pram. He is reading the newspaper.*

REGGIE. Come on . . . You're on in ten minutes and apparently it's vital you're finished by three o'clock because according to *The Times* that's when Churchill's going to speak. What a day!

ROSALIND. I've solved the welly crisis! We can stuff the toes with newspaper and they'll be as snug as toast.

REGGIE. Hey! I was going to read those!

They start to stuff their wellies. ROSALIND *holds a section of the paper.*

ROSALIND. Hang on . . . Has everyone checked the list before . . .

CHARLIE. It's all over, you dingbat, we don't ever have to do that any more, thank God . . .

JOCELYN. Imagine how awful to have got the whole way through the war and then to fall at the last fence . . . oh dear.

HETTY *returns with some umbrellas. A bell rings out.*

REGGIE. Come on, only five minutes till you're on . . . Just two more things . . . the village wondered if you wouldn't mind posing for our own bit of cinema history to show the boys when they come home . . . and they've given you this bottle of . . . something.

They cheer.

HETTY. Well, then I think this would be a good moment for a VE Day toast . . . Here's . . . to all those extraordinarily brave men who fought so that evil should not prevail.

JOCELYN. And for our children to have a future . . .

REGGIE. And here's to all the women who stepped into the men's shoes . . .

CHARLIE. Wellies . . . And proved that women are capable of doing exactly the same work as men . . .

HELEN. And now we have to give it all back to them . . . and take up crochet again . . . So here's to our time as men . . . just this once . . . to the strange, exhilarating liberty of it all . . .

ROSALIND (*winking at* CHARLIE). Some of us have no intention of giving it all back . . .

HELEN. Oh God, you two, honestly . . . I know, I know, I promised . . . as long as I don't have to read *The Well of Loneliness* . . .

FLORA. And here's to absent friends who we have so much loved and will never never be forgotten . . .

They all take a drink from the bottle.

GERTRUDE. I also have some toast to make . . .

FLORA. A toast . . .

GERTRUDE. Yes . . . of course . . . I am a refugee who has been given a home in your country . . . For which I'm thanking you all from the deep of my heart . . .

HETTY. It is us who should be grateful for all you've brought to us . . .

GERTRUDE. And I would like to say thank you most profoundly to the Hetty and the Flora . . . because they are not just the steel and the wire, they are the fire and the ice and the pollen and the bees . . . I have lost both a husband and son and someone I would have been proud to call my daughter . . . may she forgive a foolish mad old woman . . . but they produced this baby . . . and I believe she is a beautiful thing to come out of these terrible times . . .

REGGIE. Hear hear . . . Oh bless her . . . she has no mother or father . . .

FLORA. She has many mothers.

HETTY. At the very least.

GERTRUDE. Yes indeed . . . Hetty and Flora and I . . . we have chosen a name for the baby – she is to be called Bliss Rosenbaum . . .

REGGIE (*tearfully*). Oh wonderful! Spot on . . . And you know, if ever she needs a male shoulder . . . I mean avuncular advice and all that . . .

FLORA *gives him a little hug and a hanky. They stand in a circle around the pram.*

HETTY. The future of Britain belongs to you, little one . . . and to those that follow after . . . and I believe they'll look back on this time with pride and tenderness . . .

REGGIE. Quick . . . immortal moments on celluloid . . . eat your heart out, David Lean . . .

He puts down the newspaper, and takes a Union Jack and his cine-camera out of the pram. They all pose a few times, laughing and mock-serious.

HETTY. Now remember that in the cricket clothes, we're English soldiers and how do we tell the audience we are now in the French camp?

She puts up an umbrella. Laughter.

Not very appropriate but . . .

A bell rings. They start to exit.

FLORA. This is it . . . Once more unto the breach, dear friends.

HETTY*'s eye is caught by the paper. She picks it up.*

HETTY. Now remember the most important thing is to . . .

She stops abruptly as the others exit mock-fighting. She stares at the 'list'.

ALL. To tell the story . . .

ROSALIND. And to remember that whatever Olivier did, we can do better . . .

HELEN. Bless his little pudding-bowl haircut . . .

JOCELYN. Oh, apparently it's going to chuck it down with rain.

FLORA. Which will be alright when we're French . . . Hetty? Hetty?

The bell rings louder and more persistently. FLORA *runs off.*

HETTY *folds up the page, puts it next to her heart, and follows.*

JOCELYN *as Chorus comes on wearing the Union Jack.*

JOCELYN (Chorus). O! For a muse of fire, that would ascend
    The brightest heaven of invention;
    A kingdom for a stage, princes to act,
    And monarchs to behold the swelling scene . . .
    O pardon! Since a crooked figure may
    Attest in little place a million;
    And let us, ciphers to this great accompt,
    On your imaginary forces work . . .

    It starts to rain. The umbrellas go up as they enter as the
    French.

HELEN (Charles). 'Tis certain he hath passed the river Somme.

ROSALIND (Constable).
    And if he be not fought withal, my lord,
    Let us not live in France; let us quit all,
    And give our vineyard to a barbarous people.

FLORA (Britanny).
    Mort Dieu, ma vie! If they march along
    Unfought withal, but I will sell my dukedom
    To buy a slobbery and a dirty farm
    In that nook-shotten Isle of Albion.

HELEN (Charles).
    Up, Princes, and, with a spirit of honour edged
    More sharper than your swords, hie to the field.
    Now forth, Lord Constable, and Princes all,
    And quickly bring us word of England's fall.

    The play arrives at the Crispin's Day speech.

HETTY (Henry V). If we are marked to die, we are enough
    To do our country loss, and if to live,
    The fewer men, the greater share of honour.
    God's will, I pray thee, wish not one man more
    This day is called the feast of Crispian.
    He that outlives this day, and comes safe home,
    Will stand a-tiptoe when this day is named,
    And rouse him at the name . . . at the name of . . .

    HETTY *stops . . . She can't go on. They all take up the next*
    lines and pass the baton between them.

FLORA. . . . at the name of Crispian.
     He that shall live this day, and see old age,
     Will yearly on the vigil feast his neighbours,
     And say 'Tomorrow is Saint Crispian.'

CHARLIE. Then will he strip his sleeve and show his scars . . .
     And say 'These wounds I had on Crispian's day.'

JOCELYN. Old men forget; yet all shall be forgot
     But he'll remember, with advantages,
     What feats he did that day.

ROSALIND. Then shall our names,
     Familiar in his mouth as household words,
     Be in their flowing cups freshly remembered.

HELEN. This story shall the good man teach his son,
     And Crispin Crispian shall ne'er go by,
     From this day to the ending of the world,
     But we in it shall be remembered . . .

FLORA. We few.

CHARLIE and JOCELYN. We happy few.

HETTY. We band of brothers.
     For he today that sheds his blood with me
     Shall be my brother; be he ne'er so vile,
     This day shall gentle his condition;
     And gentlemen in England now abed
     Shall think themselves accursed they were not here,
     And hold their manhoods cheap whiles any speaks
     That fought with us upon Saint Crispin's day.

*The women raise their swords and freeze. Loud pealing
church bells ring out and mix with the sound of VE Day
celebrations, fragments of Churchill, etc. The sound
becomes an orchestrated version of 'I Vow to Thee, My
Country', as the set returns to a costume store. The women
take off their costumes, hang them up and dress back into
their normal clothes – dresses and skirts for all (except
ROSALIND and CHARLIE in suits and hats) . . .*

*At the climax of 'I Vow to Thee', music then cuts to a simple
piano theme and the lights change. ROSALIND and*

CHARLIE *quietly disappear through a costume rail into the darkness – then* HELEN *and* JOCELYN *– and then* FLORA, GERTRUDE *and the baby – all walk out of the light and into the dark.* HETTY *is left alone.*

HETTY. Our revels now are ended. These our actors,
As I foretold you, were all spirits, and
Are melted into air, into thin air.
And, like the baseless fabric of this vision,
The cloud-capped towers, the gorgeous palaces,
The solemn temples, the great globe itself,
Yea, all which it inherit, shall dissolve.
And, like the insubstantial pageant faded,
Leave not a rack behind. We are such stuff
As dreams are made on; and our little life
Is rounded with a sleep.

She walks slowly back through the costume rails. The lights are fading. Everything in the wardrobe store is as it was before.

The End.

Production Note

The first version of *We Happy Few* was presented at Malvern Theatres thanks to the extraordinary galvanising powers of Nic Lloyd and Serena Gordon. We had a wonderful time and we were all very proud of the production but I felt I had devised a clumsy narrative device (centring on a modern boy discovering the history of his grandparents) – one, moreover, that required the poor boy playing Joseph to change between characters at an impossible speed.

Even so, many people told me that I had written a wonderful play for amateur dramatic companies because it had generous parts for a man, a boy and a large group of women of varying ages – a story that centred on a group of amateurs with a passion for theatre – and it could be done with twelve chairs, three costume rails, some home-made costumes and a hefty reliance on the willing suspension of disbelief.

The play has changed since then – and for the West End was given a story-theatre production with all the magic that Trevor Nunn, John Napier and David Hersey have been bringing to theatre for an astonishing number of years.

However, I think the play is still eminently performable on a small budget with two planks and a passion, so to speak. It could even be done with twelve chairs around a playing circle, and an assortment of hats. Obviously the saxophone and piano can be pre-recorded, lights and sound can be used to change atmosphere and location (even torches), and costumes and props can be minimal or hinted at. It could be re-invented in many and varied ways as long as there is a consistency in the story-theatre rules invented for the production.

Whatever the case, the Shakespeare/Artemis motto 'On your imaginary forces work' should accompany any production of *We Happy Few*.